WOMAN OF EXCELLENCE

Not Without A Struggle

To: Viola
and Ravin
Best Wishes always.
With love
Carolyn Murphy

Carolyn Bell Murphy

AuthorHouse™
1663 Liberty Drive
Bloomington, IN 47403
www.authorhouse.com
Phone: 1-800-839-8640

First published by AuthorHouse 9/27/2010

ISBN: 978-1-4490-2894-7 (sc)

Library of Congress Control Number: 2010901178

Printed in the United States of America
Bloomington, Indiana

This book is printed on acid-free paper.

Edited by
Authorhouse

Book Cover designed by Oscar Murphy
www.OscarMurphyDesignGroup.com

Acknowledgments

This book is dedicated to my father and mother, who wanted the best for all eight of their children and tried to make it happen, Mrs. Hattie Kate Jackson Bell and the late Reverend Dwight Leon Bell.

To my brother, who shared my secrets, the late Dwight Leon Bell, Jr.

To my two sisters, Wynnifred Bell Frazier and Eleanor Bell Cooper; and my brothers, Will Oliver, Sterling James, Clarence and Edmond. Thank you for all you have done to brighten my life.

To my four children whose forgiveness I am asking for imposing such a horrible life on them. They deserved better. To Oscar B., III (Os), D'Vorolyn M. Murphy Talley (Voe), Sharolyn L. Murphy, Esq. (Sharol), and Wendolyn D. Murphy Cousin (Wendy).

To my six grandchildren, always make good choices. To Docia D. Murphy Johnson, Tiffany R. Murphy, Jamerel X. Talley, Javaughn M. Talley, Karolyn M. Cousin, and Evan T. Cousin.

To my first great-grandchild, Armani Kaniah Johnson, you have a big responsibility to be a positive role model for the future great-grandchildren. I know you will handle it like a champ.

To the five women who helped me launch Women of Excellence NWAS, Inc., Leonora Solomon, Barbara Pennington, Marty Bushy, Esq., Janice Baldwin, and Jessie Peterson.

To all my nieces because of the leadership I see in all of you. I hope this book will aid in your decision making. To Asonya Bell Dorsey, Karen Bell Anderson, Yvette Frazier Whiteside, Annette D. Frazier, Hope Cooper, Portia L. Bell, Latarsha S. Bell Adams, Carbietene R.

Bell, Rachel Bell, Temika L. Carter, Chrystal Carter Dorion, and Antoinette R. Bell.

To Annie Lewis, my former neighbor, longtime friend, and guardian angel.

To Brenda Coleman, a co-worker who supplied me the books to record my manuscript when I retired.

To my three first cousins Bertha Hall Dunlap, Amelia Hall Dawson, and Mary Hall Johnson, who grew up with us and watched out for us.

And to the late Mrs. Cammie Little, my favorite teacher who was also my elementary school principal. She was a risk-taker in the 1940s with admirable leadership skills, and she was always so well dressed.

Contents

PART I GROWING UP ON THE TRAVIS PLACE

Chapter 1 **3**
In the Beginning 3
Experiencing Love and Building a Solid Foundation 4
Early School Start 6
Ashamed of Where I Lived, Including Some Major Dislikes 8
My New Walk with God 12
Great Expectations 18
Some of Life's Little Lessons 19
A First for Dad that Opened Doors for Others 21

Chapter II **24**
A Time of Growth and Disappointment 24
High School Days 24
Saying Goodbye to the Travis Place Was Easy 26

PART II A WORLD I DIDN'T KNOW EXISTED

Chapter III **31**
An Awakening 31
The Beginning of a Secret Life, I Didn't See It ComingIt Took Me over Forty Years to Begin Sharing It with the World 33
Not Prepared for This—Country Girl and City Boy 35
He Had Total Control 37
Independent Thinker and Self Assured, What Happened? 39
A Change in Plans 41
Home from the Military 43

PART III WASHINGTON DC BECOMES HOME
Unhappiness Comes for a Lengthy Visit 47
A Job—I Thought the Worst Was behind Us 48
Oscar Gets a Job 49
New Beginnings and Another Baby 50
The Beginning of the Bells' Family Plan 51
A Combination of Good and Bad for the Family 52
Friends at the Post Office 54
I Got Hired at the Federal Bureau of Investigation 55
A Visit from My In-laws 56
Back to Work for Me 57

PART IV MOVE TO YOUNGSTOWN, OHIO

Chapter V 61
Introduced to Another World 61
Our Own House 63
Using His Mom's Death to Manipulate 65
Self Inventory and Counseling 66
My First Job in Youngstown, Ohio 67
Clarence Robinson Day Care Center 68
An Outing That Caused Life-threatening Consequences 70
A New Trend 71
Our First Car 72
Al-Anon 73

PART V "I CAN DO ALL THINGS THROUGH CHRIST WHICH STRENGTHENS ME"(PHILIPPIANS. 4:13, KJV).
A Church Home 77
A Virtuous Woman Described 79
Continued Visible Growth 81
The Murphy's House Was the Place to Go 83
Satan Raises His Head 86
A Major Step up for the Agency 87
Office Relocated—Something Good Happened? 91

What an Imagination 93
A Shakeup in Associated Neighborhood Centers 95
Our Son Leaves Home 96
Something Bad Got Worse 96

Chapter VII **97**
A New Start that Lasted until Retirement 97
Monumental Changes 99
Hard Work Paying Off 99
The Big Layoff 100
Called Back To Work 101
A Thought for Goal Setters 102
Transfer to the Fabrication Plant 103
A Move to the Safety Department 105
A Recognition That Led to Some Pride 107
A Day of Reckoning, I Wondered if the Change That I Wanted Would Ever Happen 109

PART VI THE UNVEILING OF MY SECRET LIFE

Chapter VIII **113**
The Move that Changed My Life Forever and I Unveiled My Secret Life 113
Life after Abuse 115
What Will Mom and Dad Say? 116
Retirement for Oscar 119
Visits from the Children 120
Retirement and Move for Me 121
Oscar's Death 122
The Funeral 123
A Decline in My Parent's Health 124
Multiple Deaths Close Together 126
Absorbed in Thought Again, Recall – Noticing Abuse Early 127
Women's Conference 129

PART VII MAKING A DIFFERENCE

Chapter IX **133**
The Beginning of Women of Excellence NWAS, Inc. 133
Some of the Rewards from the Organization 136
Intimate Moments with God 138
My Favorite Scriptures for Intimate Moments with God 140
My Special Project 141
An Ongoing Visual Aid in Schools—an Organization/Club 141
Suggestions for Implementation of an Organization/Club 142

Educational Information, Lesson Plan and Tools to Work With for Globalization Against Abuse Toward Women **143**

Epilogue **158**

Introduction

My life wasn't always a secret life that I was ashamed of and hated. I was twenty years old, and after a well-structured childhood, my life turned somewhat dreadful and caused a long journey that I hope to help other women to avoid taking.

As you read this book, you will see two great parents, leaders and one great team—my mother, who I call Mom, and my father, who I called Dad. You will see two people who loved each other and showed it for many years. As a team, you will see the good foundation they put together, supported jointly and lived what they taught before the family to show that it was the right thing to do.

I hope someone in the family will write a book on our entire family detailing the beginning with slavery, our survival, great contributions to society, and successes of the Bell family. My great grandfather was born in slavery, and the slaves were freed when he was only two years old.

If your story is at the beginning of the book, be thankful. There are many women or families who are not as fortunate as you are. To experience family love is a good thing. You will have a support group for life; they are there through the good times and the bad. They see your faults, pray for you, and still love you unconditionally.

If you see yourself throughout the pages of the second portion of the book, which depicts my secret life with major struggles, you may not be as fortunate as I was, because in too many cases, some lives are destroyed beyond repair—sometimes even to death. As I share the story of my secret life, you will see that my knowing God was never a secret! You will discover how foreign living outside Livingston, Alabama, will become for me. And finally, when I discover this new world, you may ask yourself, *why did she live a secret life so long?* If you are an abuse survivor, you might understand and know why the struggle lasted so long. Was it love, pity, embarrassment, or fear? What would make a woman stay in an abusive relationship for forty years? It wasn't a one-time abusive incident; it was an intense, ongoing, abusive relationship. It took me years to complete a goal that I started out to do when I left home, but it didn't stop me from achieving other goals. I earned over thirty-three certificates in different areas of expertise before I got my major goal accomplished and I have become a professional student as a result of this long delay. At seventy-two years old, I still take a class occasionally and oversee many conferences. If I sit down with a counselor, there may be enough hours for even a PhD. Most of my certificates were not earned in one day; they were accelerated classes that expanded from days to months. What victims of abuse call honeymoon days during the forty years together were outstanding but didn't bring true happiness because I walked on egg shells for survival and to avoid setting my abuser off. You will see that the changes I was hoping for never came. The abuse never stopped no matter how hard I tried to keep it from happening.

You will see that the serious talks were only empty promises; you will wonder after coming from such a loving family how I could settle for so little for myself and my children. There was always the idea that he could be changed. I completed my major goal—a degree—but it took years. The big wedding that I was promised never happened.

I moved into my own apartment two months before our fortieth wedding anniversary, and we became friends toward the end. When I say friends, I mean we were civil to each other because of the wonderful family we were so proud of—four children and six grandchildren. We came together and enjoyed family functions, and I would pick my husband up sometimes to give him a ride to church. I never wanted to be his wife again once I left our dream house.

When my husband had a stroke, I took him to my apartment and took care of him until he was well enough to go home. I never felt at ease in his presence. He wanted to talk about getting back together, but I would always change the subject and end by saying, "Let's get you well so you can go home." In the end, when I concluded that something had to be done to reach other women, I was given the idea to start an organization after attending a weekend conference. There is nothing magical but some common sense things that are pertinent when you get serious about doing something to end such an awful life. First, you have to realize that God created both of you, and He wants both of you to be happy. Once you stop making excuses for the abuser's actions, it will hit you—I deserve the desires of my heart also and not to be controlled by such an awful force. I also want the world through the department of education, churches, and communities to pass down to middle school principals and high school principals, colleges, universities, and other avenues to take a serious look and move on the section for raising awareness about verbal and physical abuse at an early age. It is seen in the home and oftentimes accepted as a way of life. The children consider this normal behavior because Mom accepted this behavior. Raising awareness at an early age will not stop all the abuse, but it will surely minimize it. The signs are there–children nervous about abuse and falling asleep in class because Dad fought Mom last night and they were afraid to go to sleep. If the signs are recognized, I believe someone will notice and the information will fall on fertile ground.

While traveling this journey, I have found out that another person does not create your happiness, you do, and true happiness comes from God by way of love, wisdom, and knowledge.

Christian women, stop praying for the abuser to change. You make the necessary changes for yourself. God will give you opportunities to walk through the door for change or another alternative. I don't know what He will recommend for you, but recognize the opportunities and move on them.

Wealthy women, the power and prestige that you think you have are not worth the sacrifices if you are unhappy and fearful all the time. You don't have power over the abuser.

Women who are in a relationship with law enforcement abusers, stop allowing him to manipulate the system and make you look stupid. Keep a paper trail or a diary. Don't shut up until you are heard.

Law enforcement, stop ignoring home abuse/terrorism that is going on with the people we love, care for, sleep with, and share our lives with.

Women, it is not a good life for anyone. I hope you will recognize God's strength shown in me throughout the struggle. When you have finished this book, I hope abuse, whatever form, will not be someone else's business, but our business. Women of Excellence NWAS, Inc., is a good organization where you can start the healing. Visit the website at www.womenofexcellencenwas.org. Start a group, help get the awareness class in schools, and join me as we declare war on physical and verbal abuse at home and abroad. You will find some educational tools to help with this endeavor as I wrap things up.

In the end, you will see how pleased and happy I am that I didn't let my situation dictate my praise toward God because I never would have made it without Him. Never! Thank You, God, and thank you for allowing me to share my story with you!

Part I

Growing Up on the Travis Place

Chapter 1
In the Beginning

On August 2, 1937, in Sumterville, Alabama, Reverend and Mrs. Dwight Leon Belle welcomed their first child, a daughter, Carolyn Jean Belle. Mom and Dad lived in Livingston, Alabama, but she went back home to give birth to her first child. This is what happened in some families in the earlier years. Ma Fannie, Mom's mother, wouldn't have had it any other way than for her to come back home for one month.

Our family consisted of, on Mom's side of the family, Henry Jackson and Fannie Brown Jackson, first generation from slavery who had fourteen children, with mom being the youngest girl. She is the only one still living. We called Mom's parents Pa Henry and Ma Fannie.

On Dad's side of the family were Edmond Belle and Lula Brown Belle (Mama Lula), first generation from slavery. They had two sons, and dad was the eldest. His mother died in childbirth with his brother, Robert. Edmond Belle later married Estelle Hall Belle. We called them Papa and Big Ma Kit.

Over a period of approximately sixteen years after I was born, there were a total of eight children, Dwight Jr., Will Oliver, Wynnifred, Eleanor, Sterling, Clarence, and Edmond. This is where my solid foundation began. I first saw the experience of love in such an electrifying way between two people—Dwight Leon Belle and Hattie Kate Jackson Belle. Our last name ended with an e, but at some time down through the years, we became Bell. This special kind of love has extended to me and all my siblings and it is there today.

Experiencing Love and Building a Solid Foundation

We were Mom and Dad's pride and joy. We were shown love, and nobody had children quite like Mom and Dad's. Aside from showing love for us, they showed love for each other. I would see them kiss briefly on the cheek, and he would pat her on the hips as he passed her at times. If they argued, it was not in front of us. We were told by Dad that he prayed to God to just let him live until all his children were grown because he had a very hard time when he was growing up. His mother died when he was short of two years old during the birth of his brother. He told us about the awful beatings he got for nothing, although the man who raised him was his uncle. He said his uncle would beat his aunt the way he did him, and one night he beat her and tied her outside of the house all night. She got sick with a cold and became very ill.

My dad was a kind, loving man, funny and very giving. When he went away to preach, he would bring us something back and something special for Mom. I would say, "I want a husband like Mom's, but I don't want him to be a preacher because there would be too much work to do, such as ironing all those white shirts for him and he being away from home, although it was seasonal."

It was in the summer when Dad was away a lot, after the crops were planted and waiting to be harvested. During this time, churches would have revival, and there were several churches having revival. There were so many churches because of transportation. It seemed as if every plantation had two or three churches. Walking, horseback riding, and wagons were the only means of transportation. Revival is when each church had a week of night services and three days of services during the day. In the church, there were seats set aside for sinners right up front. (Sinners were defined as people who had not accepted Christ as their Savior.) The services were so good; it seemed as if the heavens opened up. People came to support each other. There were times when members who had moved away to other cities came back home for their church's revival week. The purposes of the revivals were to revive the Christians and to bring sinners to repentance.

In revival is when we left the field early to get ready for church. Revival was at night and lasted a week at each church in the area. This is when you knew who the best preachers were. My dad would start preaching in June and preached every week until the end of August. This went on for years. Some area preachers brought preachers from out of town and some used my dad for their revival. The church was always packed, and on Friday night some of the white people came to worship with us.

When Dad went to do revival for a week at another church, to make sure he looked his best, Mom would pin everything together that she wanted him to wear. If she wanted him to wear a navy suit, she would take this big safety pin and pin his matching socks and tie to it. He always wore a white shirt and had plenty of white ironed handkerchiefs. She took pride in all those white shirts she ironed with a smoothing iron that you had to heat in the fireplace. She would brag that she ironed thirteen white shirts and all the children's clothes and none of them were burned. She made starch for our clothes from water and flour cooked on the stove. She would dip them in the solution, let them dry on line, and then bring them in, and on the day she was going to iron them, she sprinkled them with water and rolled them until it was time for them to be ironed. She would sprinkle our clothes with the starch and rolled them up until she got ready to iron them. Aside from ironing all those clothes so Dad could look good in front of people, we also looked clean and crisp. Mom even ironed our bed linen and Dad's and the boys' underwear, as if she didn't have enough to do.

Early School Start

I liked the way Mom had taught us at home when we were little. Before we became school age, we were taught to read, count, and color within the lines. When school started, I was excited about going to school, and I found out that the other children couldn't do the same things I could do. I wondered why they couldn't do the same things, especially coloring within the lines. We didn't have kindergarten back then and you waited until you were six years old to go to school. I was ready much earlier and the year I became five years old in August, I started to school that September. Dad talked to Mrs. Cammie Little about me starting to school. She told him that she would write to Mr. Malone, the school superintendent, and I could come until she heard from him. The first day I went to school, the class had to read from a book about Jack and Jill. We read about four pages and were told how many to study for the next day. I kept getting up and telling the teacher that I could read the whole book. Each time she would say, "Go sit down." Finally after school, she asked my cousin, Mary Hall, to wait for me. She wanted to see if I could read the entire book. I read the entire book and got a book with paragraphs and chapters. I was so excited, and when I got home Mom and Dad were excited too. I remember the book being very hard, but I was reading it in no time.

We didn't know what Mr. Malone was going to say about me staying in school, so we waited with apprehension. We had a lot of learning materials, such as books, the big crayons, big pencils, and writing tablets with the wide lines and a dotted line in the middle of each line to separate the capital letters from the lowercase letters. Mom didn't play. If you didn't pay attention, there was a switch sitting in the corner to remind you that it was learning time. I continued to study long hours when I got home and finished my chores. Everything traveled slowly in those days. While waiting to hear from Mr. Malone, I had added to my "Now I Lay Me Down to Sleep" prayer or the Lord's Prayer at night. I don't remember which one I was saying at that time, but I started asking God to let Mr. Malone say yes. I made a lot of promises to God about studying hard and keeping up with the other children. Finally, one day, which was much too long for us, we finally got our answer—I could stay.

Mom and Dad would get up early. In the winter time, Dad started a fire in the fireplace and tried to keep it from going out during the night. Most of the time, he tried to keep the fire going throughout the night to keep the house from getting chilled. He didn't want the children to get sick. My brother, Will Oliver, had asthma, and he wanted to make sure he didn't catch a cold. Mom would get up next, heat water for us to clean up, and cook breakfast. We had a full breakfast every morning. There were grits, something called strick of lean, ham, or sausage when we ate. There were always hot biscuits to go with our meal made from scratch. There were molasses on the table to go with our breakfast if we didn't have or want grits. There wasn't a large variety, but we were full and ate together every morning. Dad would instruct Mom to put all the food in the center of the table and let all of us eat until we were full. Usually there was a very little or anything left, but we were full. Mom packed lunches while the school-age children finished dressing and made sure we had our books and homework.

Ashamed of Where I Lived, Including Some Major Dislikes

The Travis Place was miles from nowhere in the woods but still in Livingston, Alabama. This is where we lived until two years after the eighth child was born. There were three other families who lived further down than we did. We were share-croppers, and I could tell that my dad did not like living on Travis Place. I think he stayed there as long as he did because he couldn't afford to move us and my grandfather and step-grandmother. I did not like that we lived so far back in the woods and had to walk miles to get to anywhere or rode in a buggy or wagon pulled by horses. We learned to ride a horse with or without a saddle and were not afraid. We did not leave the farm where we lived other than to go to church, school, take some neighbor something, or to do chores for some old people, as they were referred to at the time.

Another dislike was our chores. We thought they were hard at first, but we got used to them. All of us had to do these chores as we became of age. Since I was the oldest, it seemed as if no one else would ever get old enough to help me and Dad with them. There were no deviations from the chores. During the school year the chores consisted of sawing and chopping wood for cooking and for the fireplace. I learned to do both. We had to walk long distances to a spring to get enough water for drinking and to heat for baths. When one spring dried up, Dad would walk and find another. The springs were in low levels with the water coming out of the ground. Then one day, my grandfather got someone to help him dig a well. That was a blessing because we could stop those long walks down the hill and back again and again. Sometimes we would take a large container that would hold more than one bucket full and it would require team work because it needed two people to carry one container.

As time passed and as we were getting older, we started sharing chores. I still didn't like them because we had a long walk to and from school. This was the routine: We came home from school, changed our school clothes, and washed our hands first, because no one came to Mom's table without washing their hands. Afterwards, we ate a hot, delicious dinner that was missing meat sometimes, but we got full, did chores, did our homework, put our clothes out for the next day, and got ready for bed. Our clothes were always ironed and hanging on a nail behind a door of the room we slept in. Mom would dim the lights, and we went to bed at the same time. We said our prayers according to our age. The youngest children said, "Now I Lay Me Down to Sleep" and the older children said the Lord's Prayer found in Matthew 6:9–13. We learned Psalm 23, the Ten Commandments as written in Exodus 20:3–17, and John 3:16 early in life. I loved to read. Sometimes I would get a flashlight and hide under the bed and read once we were told to go to bed. I read the Bible and would learn verses for each letter of the alphabet and sometimes at the end of the year I would have read the entire Bible

Dad and Papa were fishermen and hunters. My brothers were taught to hunt and fish at an early age. They fished with nets and hooks. I fished with a hook and still enjoy it. Several times my dad and grandfather would catch fish that weighed over ninety pounds by using a net in a river. We would sit in a skiff (small boat) and sit there for hours listening to the voices of the wild. Late in the evening or very early in the morning, we enjoyed the stillness while we waited for some movement on our hooks or felt the net move. No one said a word for fear of running the fish away. Most of the time, the nets were left overnight. Papa, Dad, and sometimes my brothers would get up early to check the nets. They usually came back with big smiles on their faces and showing off the catch. There were times when they didn't have anything, but they enjoyed the sport.

In the summer and up until the second or third week in June, our chores consisted of tilling the soil, planting the crops, chopping the grass away, planting flowers, and having the prettiest yard for miles that a very few people got to see because of where we lived, and then we got a break until mid-August. Before we got old enough for these chores, we would lie on the ground and look for four-leaf clovers for hours. I would pull up some kind of grass that grew near the pond with long roots and I would tire a string around the grass just below the roots for the space to look like a head. I would then curl or braid the roots and tie ribbons on the braids or in the curls. I would line them up and read to them. We would also shoot marbles, play jacks, jump rope, pitch horseshoes, and make swings that hung from branches on trees with a rope and an old car tire and go for walks. As we got older, during the down time, we sewed and made new clothes for church and school. I learned to sew, crochet, knit, and help Mom do our hair. My sister Wynnifred, later, as she got older learned to cook. My sister Eleanor, who was much younger than I, much later learned to cook and sew. Even though we made pretty clothes, my mom didn't let us forget that her mother taught her that clothes do not make the person, the person makes the clothes. We had church clothes that we didn't dare wear to school unless there was an assembly.

We only had one sewing machine, and while one person was making clothes, my mother canned vegetables and fruits from the crops for the fall and winter. We did crafts and made pretty things for the house. Mom made us dolls and showed us how to sew without a pattern. The women in the community got together and made quilts for the winter. My brothers took small wagons and made them look like cars and put together model airplanes. We also read the Bible, hymn books, comic books, and other books that my grandfather would get from his white friend when he went to town. His friend's name was Mr. Tartt Mellon. He would have stacks of books for us. I found out later that they didn't sell magazines to Negroes until they were out of date, once a year to use as wallpaper. I remember using books for wallpaper, and we made sure the pretty pictures were always visible. We were blessed because all of ours were not outdated.

Other favorite times were Sunday mornings when we went to church and attended BYTU (Baptist Youth Training Union), which was held on Sunday evenings. Our BYTU was right after church because the congregation had too far to travel to go home and come back. Ninety-nine percent of the congregation traveled by horseback or in wagons. I also loved Vacation Bible School. I was the first child in our household to become a Christian at ten years old. I loved God, I understood salvation, and I had a miraculous experience. We were having revival in the day and night, in the morning Wednesday through Friday and at night Monday through Friday. It was very special for me this time; I knew my prayers would be answered. On Wednesday morning I asked my parents if I could go to church. I was told no because Dad wanted us to finish some spot in the field. Thursday morning came, I had been praying and I kept asking if I could go to church that morning because I wanted to join the church. Dad said, "You are too young." Something happened and I started crying. It must have been a different cry because he looked so amazed and said, "All right!" He must have felt something too. In the past if I cried because I couldn't do something, it didn't make him change his mind. I went to church and when the preacher, Reverend T. J. Thompson, finished preaching, I became so emotional. I went right up and extended my hand. He grabbed my hand and my cousin Edmond Kimble (Buddy) joined me at the altar, where we both became emotional. This was the beginning of a new life for me.

Finally, before I go on, my major dislike as I grew older was when I began to notice that we were sharecroppers. Being a sharecropper didn't mean that the harvest would be shared equally between the owner and the tenant but it meant that the property owner got his share first. If there was a drought or a lot of rain through out the summer, it would cause all the crops to do very poorly. It caused some of the farmers to be very sad because they knew how dreadful things would be throughout the winter months. I saw sadness on my grandfather's face like you wouldn't believe as he would go out and look over the crops. For example, when it was time to pick cotton after a bad summer, the owner got the first bail of cotton and many times there was not enough for a full second bail. Cotton was the biggest money maker.

My New Walk with God

Coupled with Some Minor Family Challenges

This new walk with God gave me a new lease on life. When I got this new beginning, it allowed me to take the good with the bad with ease. The things that I hated doing didn't bother me anymore. Filling in at church and volunteering didn't bother me anymore. Helping the elderly in the church was a pleasure. My dad was always teased about how emotional he got when he baptized me, his first child. As my siblings understood salvation, we joined the church and Dad was the one who baptized us because he was the pastor. He baptized all eight of us. We never missed church unless we were very ill. It was a part of our life. As the preacher's kids, it was expected of us. We were the role models in the community. On Saturday evening we cooked Sunday's dinner and got our clothes ready for church. We did double on Saturday so we wouldn't have to do anything but go to church, eat, and wash the dishes on Sunday. That was God's day, and we didn't do chores. On Sunday morning, we went to church and came home to the best meal of the week. We dressed up and had Sunday clothes on that we didn't wear anywhere but to church. When we got home and as we changed clothes, Mom would change first and heat up the food. Dad said this long grace (we thought), and we ate this big dinner. We loved each other and showed it day after day. We fought, but if my parents knew it we would hug and makeup.

Also, in the summer, I looked forward to my cousins Yvonne and Sonny Kennedy coming home from St. Louis, Missouri. They were my Uncle Jack's grandchildren; He was my grandfather's brother on my dad's side of the family. My cousin, James Bell Jr., the son of my uncle Jimmy would come to visit us also during this time. He lived close to the city of Livingston, Alabama so he could play with them too. At night, James, who we called Junior, would go home and come back during the day. Their parents allowed them to come to visit during the month of July and the first weeks in August. The summer of 1947 was different because I was a Christian. During our leisure time, we went fishing and read books that had been given to us by Papa and some he had purchased. We also read the Bible and sang hymns. We played with dolls made from old stockings and also my favorite from a special kind of weed. We made doll clothes from pieces of material that weren't used to make quilts.

They went to Vacation Bible School with us. Mrs. Lela Travis was the director. She was a lady before her time, intelligent, creative, and with very little education, and she was grooming me to take her place. It was expected of us to fill in when someone didn't show up for any church activity. I taught my first Sunday school class at six years old. Our teacher was not there, and I read the questions from the catechism and the students gave me the answers. This was the beginning of my leadership roles. After this, at nine years old, I began teaching Vacation Bible School. The classes had to do a project every year. My class's project won first place three years in a row. After three years, the other teachers thought we should do something different or not have the projects judged. We stopped having them judged, but we still did a project and had a program where the children showed what they had learned. I surprised them with having my class do a craft or card to give their parents on the final night. My children sang and spoke so loud. I was only a child myself, and God was with me and I knew it. I wasn't proud and puffed up, but thankful. Because of my children doing so well in Vacation Bible School, it never came to my mind to be stuck up or boastful.

Near the end of August, my cousins who were visiting were always fun, and now I was sad because they had to go home to get ready for school. We began picking cotton and stripping and cutting down sugar cane. The sugar cane was taken to the molasses mill so my grandfather could turn it into molasses. We also pulled up peanuts and put them in stacks and dug up sweet potatoes and white potatoes and stored them for winter. Sometimes we didn't finish these things before school started in September, and nothing was said. It was expected that the share-cropper's children would start school late. We could hardly wait to start school. We went to the fields early and stayed late without having to be told. We also went for a half day on Saturday. Going back to school, getting away from the hours we spent in the hot sun and with new clothes, was a big treat. It was also a treat to see old friends whom we hadn't seen over the summer.

Before we left for school, Mom prayed out loud every morning. Her favorite saying was, "From early in the morning until all night, I thank You, Lord, for blessings. Take care of my husband as he goes one way and my children going another. Take care of the ones who are left here with me. Please bring everybody back again safely."

I would often say, "I'll be glad when I am old enough to leave this Travis place." Even as a child, I prayed for a better life although we were better off than a lot of families. I believed God was going to answer my prayers because we were Christians, we loved God, and we were keeping His commandments. He had healed my bother Dwight from polio, and he could walk except for a limp. That was hard and getting us away from Travis place would be easy. I remember this being my first act of faith. As stated in Hebrews 11:1 (KJV), "Now faith is the substance of things hoped for, the evidence of things not seen …" I saw better days ahead for the family. The doctor who treated my brother for polio had a daughter who also had polio. He told my parents that his daughter and my brother would always be in wheelchairs. His daughter was, but my brother walked and started to school with only leg braces. (He later went in the army and went on to live a normal life.) I knew getting away from the Travis place was much easier. I could see us someplace else. We were tired of seeing the owner's horses and cows walk through our yard and leave waste that had to be cleaned up to keep someone from accidentally stepping in it. I saw a bigger house than three bedrooms and a kitchen with ten people. I knew it was going to happen and it wouldn't be in the next life but soon.

Even in such crowded quarters, we always had a big Christmas. There was always room to squeeze a Christmas tree into the biggest room where my sister Wynnifred and I slept. Santa Claus brought dolls that Mom had made, and we also got one from the store. We had a Christmas tree that we went to the forest and cut ourselves. Mom and Dad would go downtown and purchase decorations for the tree. There were doll clothes, dishes, and other gifts. My brothers got wagons, tricycles, juice harps, and harmonicas. There were always books to read from my grandfather. We also got new everyday dishes. We ate from a tin pan and drank from a tin cup and on Sunday and holidays, we got out the pretty white dishes that were trimmed in silver with blue and yellow flowers. I loved the times when something was done special. There would always be a gift for Mom and Dad from Papa. Mom would cook eight or nine cakes and five or six sweet potato pies so she could share with anyone who came to visit. We had pecan trees and black walnut trees. Large bags of these were used for gifts also.

In our house, education was stressed. It was a big thing. My great-grandmother, Bettie Belle, went to college and taught for fifty-three years before retiring. After retiring, she started the first nursery school in Sumter County. It was called the Little School. She kept and taught the children of teachers who worked at the elementary and high school. My dad completed the tenth grade, but when he was called to preach, he was determined to get further education. He studied, and he loved to read. He went to Selma University in Selma, Alabama, and majored in theology and received a certificate. He had an astounding vocabulary and was always reading and keeping up with current events. Mom stopped in the eleventh grade because of the distance she had to walk to high school—seven miles to and from school. She went to school in the dark and came home in the dark. Mom continued learning and writing poems and speeches. She also wrote letters for the people in the community who could not read and write. She also read to them when they received mail or had something that had to be read. She taught us at home. We were told over and over, "What's in your head, no one can take it away from you." Dad would say, "I want you to have a better life than I had growing up." To the girls he would say, "I want you to be able to take care of yourself. I don't want you to date (go with) any guy who will hit you or talk to you any kind of way. Your Mom and I have done and still are doing a good job raising you, so don't take any meanness from a guy." He would go on to say, "No matter how no-good a man is, he is always looking for a good woman."

My brother, Dwight Jr., who was a year and nine months younger than me, had polio and couldn't walk, but my mom kept up his studies at home. He didn't start school until he was eight years old, but he was right with his class and graduated salutatorian. By the time he and my next brother, Will Oliver, got to the eighth and ninth grade, the owner of the land came riding up one day and called my dad. "Preacher, I want to see you." My dad said, "Yes sir." Mom and we were scared; we were looking out through our one window until Dad came back in the house. My mom asked him what he wanted. Dad said, "He told me that it is time to take the two biggest boys out of school, even though one is crippled from polio, because he has work for them to do." He told dad he needed new fences to keep his cows from getting out. The cows would walk all through Mom's pretty flowers. He also needed them to bale hay and do other things. My dad told him, "If an education is good enough for your children, it is good enough for mine, and I am not going to take my children out of school." He got on his horse, with whip in hand and rode away. We were scared for a long time because we did not know what the outcome would be. All of us could run through the woods if we had to, but my cripple brother wouldn't be able to get away. Nothing happened to us. God was with us.

There were neighbors and relatives who were not as brave as my dad when it came to taking Negro children out of school. When some parents were told that it was time to take the children out of school, they did. Up until two years ago, every time I went home, one of my cousins would say to me, "You know, I was just as smart as you were, but I had to drop out of school." I would say, yes, I know. There were three brothers, in particularly, who had to drop out of school. When we heard about it, I remember crying, other people were crying and actually sobbing. I felt so sad for a long, long time.

When my two oldest brothers graduated from high school, they went into the army, and a few years later, another brother went to college and another into the navy and the last one straight to college. Four brothers graduated from college; two got a second degree and one got a third degree. Dwight did not graduate from college but did extremely well and worked as a police officer for the postal inspection service until he retired. He received several awards and he also received professional training while in the army. He was the most gifted of all eight children.

Looking back and recalling the earlier years, things began to change for us when Mom had her eight child. My dad said, "No more, no more! With eight children my wife will not go to the fields again!" Dad had to preach for revival a week out of town and he had heard about some property being auctioned off near Sumter County Training School. He went to Mr. Tart Melon, my grandfather's white friend, and asked him to go to the auction for him because he had to go to church out of town. Mr. Melon purchased five acres of land for Dad and told him he could pay him back as he got enough money because he was in no hurry to get it back. He was able to get it for a very small amount. He told Dad the reason he got five acres was because, "You are a preacher, and I know you don't want anybody living right up under you." We were so happy, but it was a few years before he started building. Some naysayers said he would never build.

Great Expectations

Great things were expected of us, one of which was to do better in school than the other children.We were the preacher's children. After each of us started to school, it was expected of all of us because not only was Dad a pastor and Mom the supportive wife, they were both smart and had made the honor roll in school. Mom had the prettiest handwriting of most I have seen. The teachers knew that we could read, write, count, and color within the lines when we started to school. Everybody who knew us had their eyes on the preacher's kids. If we did anything that they thought or even suspected was bad, they told Mom and Dad. Sometimes if we were misbehaving and an elderly person saw us, he or she would spank us and take us home to our parents. If the elderly person didn't spank us, our parents would do so when we got home. This was true with all children during that time. Adults didn't have to be your parents to correct you.

Some of Life's Little Lessons

We were taught about salvation early in life, to have good morals and always put Christ first in our lives and let our light shine so that others will recognize it. We went to church every Sunday and at other times. It became a part of life, and it was something that I enjoyed and looked forward to doing. At an early age I found out that if you kept God's commandments, He would not only bless you, but He would also bless your children and children's children and supply all your needs according to His riches in glory and even give you the desires of your heart. How awesome, I would say. This is just what I wanted for my life because early in life, I know things happened and it had to be *God!*

It was stressed that when we were talking to someone, we should speak up, look them in the eyes, and don't act as if we were afraid of anyone. It was taught also to respect older people, always be polite, and when talking, be sure to say yes ma'am and no sir. In fact, we were taught to respect everyone and avoid burning bridges because Mom would say, "You never know who you will have to ask for a favor." She would always end it with a familiar story.

As far as appearance, I was told to always sit up straight with my back against the chair and feet flat on the floor. Mom walked with her shoulders back with her stomach pulled in until she got in her early seventies, and I followed her posture. I knew when to smile and always look my best. Another thing that we were taught early was to save some of our money and how to take care of the things we had. You first investment was to God—the first fruits and as the Lord had prospered you went to the church. The second payment was to you—put some into a savings to save for a rainy day. Dad would say, "Never live so the balance is not enough to live off," and Mom always agreed. If someone gave us some money, we saved it in a jar, under the mattress, or in a can. From the time I was in the third grade, the church got its portion and I started buying savings stamps every Monday at school and put them in a book until it was filled. When it was filled, the principal took the book to the post office and got a savings bond. On May Day, we would have a big outing at school and invite parents and the superintendent of schools. Other people were allowed to attend also. It was on May Day when the bonds were presented. (All of mine matured and gained interest, and when I went away to college they were a big help with college expenses.) I was happy to be one of the children going out on the field to get my bond or bonds. We would also do May Day dancing. The people would scream and clap when they saw the preacher's kid dancing. We also did a pattern that looked like weaving on the May pole by going over and under the next person. It was the fun thing to do in those days.

I must say right here, I didn't always follow this lesson about giving and saving over a period in my life. I strayed from this lesson and overspent many times, but I never forgot this scripture that says, "Train up a child in the way he should go: and when he is old, he will not depart from it" (Proverbs 22:6, KJV). I also taught my children these lessons, and it has paid off. I learned that it is better to give than to receive. What you give comes back to you sometimes two and three fold. I have been back on track for over forty-two years. Without hesitation, the church's check comes first.

We were also taught to take care of our clothes. The church clothes, the school clothes, and everyday clothes were separated. They were not interchangeable; they were worn when they were supposed to be worn. They were hung up and the things that were supposed to be folded were folded and put away. When we washed the clothes, they were separated according to color. The white clothes never got dingy. They would be worn until they had holes in them, but they never, never got dingy. Mom would always stress the importance of taking care of what you already have. She would say, "It is not how much you have but how well you take care of what you have." My brothers were very close in age, so they had the opportunity to pass their clothes down to the next brother.

A First for Dad that Opened Doors for Others

A Credit Card for Dad?

As time passed, Dad came up with an idea where he was going to see if he could make things easier for Mom, as he was always looking for ways to help her. I was the only girl old enough to be in school and was getting bigger, and it was taking longer to make my clothes. Mom was staying up later and later making dresses for me. During this time my sisters Wynnifred and Eleanor only needed a few dresses for church and three outfits for everyday because Mom was, it seemed, always washing. Although I had learned to do some sewing like hemming the dresses and slips, we weren't keeping up with the number of outfits she wanted for me to have for school or for my sisters for church. We had a foot peddling sewing machine that required a lot of energy. Dad noticed that in all the sewing, Mom didn't make anything for herself because she was spending all the time on us. There was a lady at our church named Mrs. Shelton who could sew, and Mom asked Dad if she asked this lady to help with some sewing would he take some material and patters over to her house to see if she would help make some dresses for the girls. Mom asked her the next Sunday at church if she could help with some sewing. She agreed and told mom that she would charge $1.50 to make each dress. We thought that was too much, but Mom needed help. When the clothes were finished, she sent them over with her husband, Mr. Frank Shelton. When he arrived, we were so excited and could hardly wait to try them on. We thought that price was too much and we didn't like the way the dresses looked, but we wore them anyway. They were all made alike but in different colors. Daddy told Mom that he wanted her to have something too. "I want you to look pretty so let me take some material over and have Mrs. Shelton make something for you. Where are your clothes?" he asked. She told him that there wasn't enough material left to make anything for her.

He wasn't happy with that answer, so he went to Sears, Roebuck & Company to open his first charge account. He drove thirty-two miles away to see if they would let him have some things on credit. He told them the story about not having enough material left for Mom to make her any clothes and there was no money left to buy anything for her. He told them that he was a preacher and he wanted his wife to have something to look good in also. It was after the crops that were harvested and cotton picked and sold that everyone did their shopping. This time, there wasn't enough for everybody. Dad was given an application to fill out. When he had finished, he was given a charge account. The salesman told Dad that if he loved his wife that much and drove that far without knowing whether he would get the account, he was going to let him have the account.

When Dad established his credit, we were allowed to get bigger things, battery radio, and a bedroom suite with all matching pieces. This opened doors for many other people to get charge accounts. Sears, Roebuck & Company welcomed the added business. They offered Dad other things like sheer silk stockings for Mom and jewelry. He was told that since dad was a preacher, his wife shouldn't be wearing those thick stockings on Sunday.

When Mr. Tartt Melon, my grandfather's white friend, heard about the silk stockings, he was happy because he had been selling them to Dad for Mom for a long time. He had been waiting for someone else to do the same thing and hoped they would do that for all women. He had been hiding them back for Mom. His store didn't have credit cards. The buyers' names were written in a book and they would subtract from the total debt when the buyers paid on the bill. I don't know if Mr. Tartt was like some of the store owners or not because I heard that some owners did more adding than subtracting. We never thought that Mr. Tartt was one of those because he was good to us. My great-grandfather told my grandfather that we were distant cousins and Mr. Tartt knew about it. I don't know if it was true, but when my grandfather on my dad's side died, he broke down and cried as much as we did. They called my grandfather Shug and he told us that Shug was the best man in the world and one of his best friends. He told us that he loved Shug and they had been friends for years. I know when my grandfather caught huge fish or killed a deer he would put them in the wagon and take them for Mr. Tartt to see. We believed him when he said he loved Papa. We loved Papa too! Papa bought me my first tube of lipstick and saved us from many whippings. Sometimes when Mom and Dad got the switch, we would run to Papa and he would grab us and shield us. There was so much love between us. I often think of the funny moments we shared together.

Chapter II
A Time of Growth and Disappointment
High School Days

In high school, I was a cheerleader and majorette but could only attend the games during the day at school. One day after we had practiced our cheers so hard, I knew my dad would take me to the night game so I took the megaphone home. I knew he wouldn't refuse to take me to the game or take me to one of my aunts and uncles' house so I could go with them. I pleaded and pleaded, and the answer was still no. The next day when I got to school, the news was out that the uncle and aunt that I would have ridden with had an accident. My uncle was hurt badly and was sick for months. When Mom and Dad heard it, I got that look, and Dad said, "God knows best and my mind does not fool me." I walked away murmuring, and he heard me. He just looked around without saying a word. I was saying it is always the same. We don't get to enjoy things like other children. I had been on the homecoming court twice and could only attend the first night game of the year. My uncle Jessie W. O. Bell, who we called Uncle Pun, lived in Detroit, Michigan, and was home visiting the second year and he took me to the homecoming dance because he was excited that I was on the court. This was also during my senior year. He embarrassed me to death trying to dance with me. He would clap his hands and do a step and jump back. The students laughed so hard, and he left and came back for me. I was so glad to be at the homecoming dance that I didn't dare refuse to dance with my uncle. My parents were happy because he took me and that way I would be there when the homecoming court came into the auditorium. On the way home he told me not to tell the preacher that he had been dancing. We both got a good laugh.

I was also allowed to go to my junior and senior prom. My dad took me to Meridian, Mississippi, to go shopping, and we selected the prettiest dress. It was a white, floor-length gown with a lot of ruffles and flowers. Dad also helped me to select the shoes and a tiny purse to match. I wore the same dress to my senior prom and changed the flowers. My dad dropped me off and picked me up. We didn't take pictures before I left home, but family came over to see the preacher's kid going off to a dance. The only negative things that were said was that I had my nails painted with the polish my grandfather had bought me with the matching lip stick. I felt so special with so much love shown toward me in preparation for these occasions.

When time came for graduation there was more than one student to graduate at the top of the class. There were only two of us who had a slight edge on the other top students. We had scored high on the statewide academic test. My high score was in history. I don't remember who the other person was who made the high score, and I was unable to find out at our fiftieth high school reunion. We were asked to bring something from our senior year to the reunion, and I took the copy of my certificate that I had received in history. It was announced over the loudspeaker when the results came back. This was the first time our school had someone in the top ten. Both of us were in the top five. At graduation, Dad was on program and the family was so proud. When I went across the stage, the principal didn't just shake my hand. He also tipped his cap as the senior advisor handed me my diploma. Dad wasn't surprised; he told me that God was answering his prayers. "All of you are going to have success stories, just wait and see," he would say. He was right.

Saying Goodbye to the Travis Place Was Easy

Saying goodbye to the Travis place was easy. I was getting ready to go away to college, and when I would return at Christmas time, the house would be finished. Mom, Dad, and I went shopping for a couple of store-bought dresses and other things to go with my homemade dresses. Dad would shop right along with us. He told Mom to get everybody something, including her. I thought she had done that, but when I went to pack, I saw a dress lying beside my footlocker that I thought was Mom's. I said to her that she had left her dress lying on the bed and asked her if she wanted me to hang it up. She told me to look at the size. I looked and it was my size. I was so happy and said, "Thanks, Mom!" Dad and Mom drove me to Stillman College in Tuscaloosa, Alabama. I listened to a sermon until I got there. We unloaded my belongings, and looked around the campus, which wasn't much. We hugged, kissed, choked up, and said goodbye.

Shortly afterward, Dad hired Mr. Samuel Madison, a builder, to build the house we needed and to get away from having to work on the Travis Place. My two oldest brothers were taking shop in school, and they, along with other classmates, built the cabinets for the kitchen. We had a large house about two and a half miles from downtown Livingston. We had dry walls painted, electric lights, and indoor plumbing came shortly afterwards. We didn't have to put wallpaper in some rooms on the walls, and Sears Roebuck catalog pages in the other rooms that no one could see but us. Before we moved, some of our relatives told my dad that if we moved where he couldn't farm, we would starve to death because we couldn't live off his salary as a pastor. He ignored the naysayers and moved anyway. When we moved, the whole community purchased property near our property and built homes also. My dad shared one of his lots with my grandfather, Edmond Bell, and step-grandmother, Estelle Bell. They moved next door. There were no share-croppers left on the Travis Place. We planted a huge garden; Dad got a job working at Livingston College in downtown Livingston. He was allowed to take off for a funeral or if he had to preach doing the week and his salary was never cut. We were blessed and lived better because Dad also preached on Sunday at the church.

We were so excited when Mom got a washing machine . It was the ringer kind. The ringer part had a handle that turned. When my step-grandmother, Estelle, noticed our new washing machine, my grandfather went and opened him an account also and bought a washing machine. The clothes still had to be hung outside, but they dried quicker because the wringer Would get rid of most of the water. Soon after wards most of the members in church had a washing machine and were able to put the tubs and washboards in the storage house.

My dad continued to pastor Shiloh for a total of twenty-eight years. He also ventured out and sought bigger churches with larger congregations. His biggest church was Ebenezer Baptist Church in Meridian, Mississippi, for thirty-four years. We were really blessed—a new home, a bigger church for Dad, and our grandfather and step-grandmother lived next door instead of down the road. We had a better-looking car than most of our neighbors and members at the church. Things were going well for the Bell family.

PART II

A WORLD I DIDN'T KNOW EXISTED

Chapter III
An Awakening

In 1954, I graduated from high school in May at age sixteen and turned seventeen in August. It was time to say goodbye to this great team, Mom and Dad, and the loving sisters and brothers that I had been with all my life. I went to Stillman College in Tuscaloosa, Alabama. I had grown up in such a sheltered environment that I didn't realize that there was a whole different world awaiting me. This was going to be the beginning for something bigger and better for the family. I was told many times that when you get your education and a job, you are to help the next sibling. I was headed off to start this beginning for a better life after living on the Travis place. I was not ready for what was about to happen. My world changed dramatically because I had never been away from home other than to spend the night with my cousins. I didn't know we were poor because we were loved. We were happy. We always had nice clothes and plenty of food to eat. On the first day of school I had an awakening like I had never had before. It seemed as if everybody had more than I had. I laugh about it now. My clothes were mostly homemade and my roommate's were all store bought. When she had finished unpacking, I noticed my roommate had shoes to match almost every outfit. I had two pair, one pair for church and one pair for school. One thing I was happy about as I was reading through the information in the room was that we had to go to church every Sunday. I didn't mind at all because this is what I was used to doing. We left the dormitory and went to a reception that was being held for the freshman.

When we got to the reception, everybody was eating and dancing and having fun. I met this guy from Spartanburg, South Carolina, named Oscar Murphy Jr. who came to greet us as we walked into the room. He was an upperclassman who the school had brought back early to greet the freshman. We became friends right away. When the dancing continued, he asked me for the first dance. He was good looking, a member of the national honor society, the most popular, the best dancer, one of the best dressed. He was also on the yearbook staff and he made sure I had a lot of pictures in the yearbook. If the upperclassmen had an event and needed a hostess, I was always asked to be one. I was my class secretary for the next two years. I also became Ms. Photographer and was nominated Miss Sophomore but someone else won. I came in second. He told me he had helped to count the votes and he was rooting for me. We remained friends three years before we started dating.

The Beginning of a Secret Life, I Didn't See It Coming
It Took Me over Forty Years to Begin Sharing It with the World

When Oscar and I started dating, I was already a cheerleader and majorette and we practiced a lot. He was always there looking, and sometimes he would sit on the steps at the gym and I wouldn't see him until I came out. On campus, if you didn't date one of the Tuckers, you were just an average person. By now we had started dating heavily and my boyfriend wasn't just a Tucker, he was the president of the Tuckers. It didn't take long to discover a Dr. Jekyll and Mr. Hyde were locked into what I thought was a smart, beautiful person. I didn't know that he was a heavy drinker and slapped his girlfriends around until the girls in the dormitory heard about us dating and told me, "Your dad is a preacher, and you can't take that guy home with you." I thought they were jealous and making up stuff because he openly had so much going for him. As stated previously, he was nominated one of the best dressed, was a member of the National Honor Society, and other things. I had never heard of young folks or teens being heavy drinkers. The people in our circle in Livingston, Alabama, were people who went to church on Sunday. I thought, *if he is, it is going to change with me.* I had no idea what I was getting into. This is when I was first accused of being naive for thinking I could change him. I saw it as another act of faith because faith is the substance of things hoped for and the evidence of things not seen, as stated from the Bible earlier (Hebrews 4:1). It took me a very long time to finally realize that they were right.

A few weeks into the relationship, he wanted to spend every minute away from class and my practices with me. We studied at the library together, went to the canteen together, met in front of the church on Sunday, and went to Vesper on Sunday evening at the church together. Things were going all right, but I wanted to spend some time with my other friends. When I finished studying and had a snack it was time to go to bed. There were times when we would just sit and say nothing for hours when we would be together. I wasn't knowledgeable about abuse, and this was my first red flag: the beginning of the silent treatment that lasted sometimes for days.

Not Prepared for This—Country Girl and City Boy

After about three or four months, I was late getting to the library and he asked me why I was late. I told him that we had more to do because I had started working in the cafeteria. This way if I didn't have money, the supervisor would give us what was left over to take to the dormitory for a snack later. He said, "You are lying." I was stunned! I just stared at him. He took my arms and twisted them up behind my back and kept asking me, "Where have you been?" I repeated the same thing; we had more to do at work. When he let go, he told me that he would die if he found out that I was seeing someone else. He apologized over and over. I forgave him and things were fine for a while. We laughed and talked. When we went to dances, we had a good time, and he was so sweet and loving. We didn't have those long silent periods where we sat and said nothing to each other.

It was our sixth month of dating. He called it our sixth anniversary. We celebrated at dinner. I wasn't hungry, so I gave him mine also. When people passed our table, he would say to them that I was so much in love, I couldn't eat. When we finished eating, he asked me to marry him. I told him I couldn't because I had one more year in school and the family had a plan. He asked me if it included him. I said, "No, because when we made the plan we didn't know you." He asked me what the plan was. I said, "My dad wants me to graduate and get a job so I can help my brother, and we will do that until everybody has graduated from college." He laughed and said, "You will be an old maid by then and nobody will want you." The sitting together and not talking lasted for days, and the not talking lasted longer this time. We were still spending all of my time away from class together. He started showing up smelling like alcohol. Some days he would be staggering and looking wild in the eyes. I told him that he had to stop drinking and he laughed. I had been so naive and sheltered and thought I would be able to change this type behavior. Had I been knowledgeable about abuse, I would have walked away after the first silent period. As you read on you will see why I have offered aid with getting the message out early about abuse.

He Had Total Control

He told me that he would be graduating in a few weeks and we were going to get married. He was going in the army, and when he got out, we could have a big church wedding. I didn't have a chance to say yes or no. He had it all planned. He had asked my first cousin Richard Hall to go with us and his roommate would drive us to Columbus, Mississippi. I said to him, "I told you about the family plan. I have got to finish school." Looking frightened, he said, "I am not going to leave you here unless we get married." He said that when he graduated he was going in the Army because he had used up all his deferments and I could stay there and finish my senior year and we could have a big church wedding when he came home from the service. As I told you, he also told me that he would be back often to visit me when he finished basic training. We went to Columbus, Mississippi, and got married.

After we got back to the campus, I went to the dean of women and asked her if I could spend the night with my friend Laura Morrison, who stayed right across the street from the school. I told Laura that Oscar and I were married and that we were going to spend the night at Mrs. Miller's house. Oscar was a good friend to her son, and they had cake and ice cream and a nice dinner prepared for us. He had told them it was going to happen and they had made plans. The next weekend my oldest brother, Dwight, came up to visit me. He asked me if I had told my brother. I said yes, but he was not going to tell anybody. He grabbed my arms and was squeezing them so tight his fingernails were digging in my flesh. My reply was, "My brother said he wasn't going to tell," and he didn't.

It was getting close to graduation and he was expecting his parents to come down for the graduation ceremony. He shared all the good things about them, and he knew that I was going to like them and they would like me. His parents came down, and I was introduced as his girlfriend. He won the award for having the highest average in his field than any other student in his class. After the graduation, when it was time to leave, he told his parents that he loved me and wanted to marry me. Jokingly, his mother was concerned about all the things that he had promised her that he was going to buy for her. He kissed me, hugged me, and when they hugged me, they left.

Independent Thinker and Self Assured, What Happened?

I went back to the dormitory and laid on my bed sobbing. It wasn't because they had gone but because of what I had done. Up until then, I had always considered myself to be an independent thinker, a self-assured person. I thought I had it going on, but now I wasn't so sure anymore. I wondered if the plan about helping each other was still going to happen. We were taught to think for ourselves and not be copycats. If we wanted something that my parents couldn't afford, Mom or Dad would say, "We don't have the money, and you don't know how they got theirs." You shouldn't always want what somebody else has. They were right, and I always felt fine afterward. We were taught to be responsible citizens and not to depend on anyone to do the thinking or things we could do for ourselves. What happened is a mystery to me. I hadn't told my parents because it was a secret. Was it love? Was I afraid of what he might do? Had I become gullible? Was I naive? I know the decisions that I had made at this time were not what I expected or wanted. I wanted a big church wedding with lots of people because I was a preacher's kid. Was I thinking at all or just following orders from someone not in authority? Was it that I didn't want to spend any more time in Livingston where the only thing to do was teach school and get married? I remembered having put some sweaters in layaway for school in a downtown store and Negroes weren't allowed to try clothes on. I spoke up and said, "Suppose they don't fit?" The owner said, "When you come to get them out, you can try them on then and exchange them." That sounded fair enough. When I finished paying for the sweaters and went to get them out, she still wouldn't let me try them on. I spoke up and repeated what she had said and stood there waiting to try them on. She called Mom and told her that I was standing there in her store being sassy. Mom told me to take the sweaters and come home. I stood up for myself and with the thought of danger, I wanted her to honor what she had told me. What had happened to me now?

I remembered the first year in English class. Mrs. Lena Lo asked the class to write a paper using our imagination and the title of my paper was, "How I Imagined the Negroes Years from Now." I also thought of all the things I talked about in the paper for example—the Negroes getting better roles in movies other than the maid and the butler. I loaded the paper up with things that I imagined being better for Negroes. It was in the fifties, and I didn't expect my teacher to react the way she did to my paper. I had no idea what the other students had imagined, but I thought my imagination was fair and reasonable. My final comment was, "I see Negroes becoming mayors, congressmen, in the senate, and one day becoming president of the United States." During the next class period when we got our papers back, we were told that when you get your paper you could leave. I noticed that everyone had their paper except me. Mrs. Lo quickly pulled a chair beside her desk and told me that she wanted to see me. She proceeded to tell me that she had asked the class to write a paper using their imagination and not this. I boldly responded by saying that I did use my imagination. I wasn't afraid and sat there as she scratched up my paper and made funny noises with her mouth. Her final words were, "It will never happen!" She continued by saying, "Do it over!" I wasn't afraid. However, I wondered what the other students imagined and why she was so bitter with my paper. The paper was almost two pages, and I imagined all of those things happening. What had happened to me? Why didn't I imagine what my life would be like with a husband or maybe a child and not be able to finish school. Whenever I was asked to take a leadership role, I had no trouble stepping right up to do so. I was a take-charge person, and now I was allowing myself to be controlled—not following but told what I was going to do. Why now, Lord, had I made such an awful decision that didn't allow me to really think about what I was getting into? I had never met his parents or any of his relatives. Was it because he was so popular in school? Whatever it was, he and his parents had gone and now I was so happy!

A Change in Plans

When they left, I was relieved; I could spend time with my friends who stayed for the summer to work. I began feeling sick every morning. I called my brother Dwight to come up. I told him what I thought was going on. I asked him not to tell. He went straight home and told our parents. Our parents called and told me to come home as soon as my work time was up. I wrote and told Oscar. He said, "I don't want you pregnant and staying there." He told me to come up and we could stay with his parents until September when he went to the army. My parents agreed and told me to make sure I came back to finish my final year of college. Even though I was expecting, I was still planning to complete my final year in school. I had gotten permission to stay on campus. I could have easily finished. He didn't want me to go back. He wanted me to stay with his parents because when he came home on leave, it would be closer. He told me to wait until he got out of service and he would be able to visit me more. I went to Youngstown, Ohio. I stayed with his parents about two months after he left for the Army. There was always an excuse for me not to go back to school. My parents were disappointed but wanted me to do what my husband had said. I was disappointed and cried for days.

One day my mother-in-law asked me to go to the store for something, and when I got back some friends were over and she had pictures of his previous girlfriend showing them. She didn't try to hide them or anything. When the friends left, she left and asked me to clean the house. I cleaned three rooms and stopped to rest. When she got back and saw I had only cleaned three rooms she called me awful names and told me how nice his previous girlfriend had been. I called my oldest brother and told him I wanted to come home. He encouraged me to come on. When I got my first check, I purchased a ticket and asked my father-in-law to take me to the bus station because I was going home and didn't want to ask Mae (my mother-in-law) to take me. He told her that I was leaving. She said she would take me to the bus station and she did. She even hugged me and told me to call her when I got home. She was never told that I was going to stop to visit Oscar. He was stationed in Louisville, Kentucky. I stopped by and spent the weekend there with him. He started talking about how fat I looked. He asked me why his parents didn't come. I told him that I wasn't going back there, I was going home. He was furious. He told me to write him every day when I got there and asked me what his mother did for me to leave. I told him how she had acted toward me when I stopped to rest after cleaning three rooms. I told him that she acted as if I was a kid and would ask me to walk to the store to get stuff when she had friends over. I don't know what she told him, but I didn't hear from him for a long time. I stayed at home and my baby (Oscar III) was born two weeks and four days early. He weighed three pounds and four ounces. I called and told him about the baby. He was so happy and wanted me to describe him. He wanted to know if I had named him Oscar III as he asked me to do. I told him yes. He said he loved us and could hardly wait to see us. We called often to give him updates on what was going on with us and what was going on with the rest of the family. Although he said he was anxious to see us, when he got leave the Christmas after the baby was born, he went to his parents' house, and we didn't see him until the next year when he was discharged from the service.

Home from the Military

He got out of the army at the end of two years. Instead of coming to where the baby and I were, he went to Spartanburg, South Carolina. He was stationed in Alaska for the last year of service, and we didn't see him until he was discharged. However, the whole two years he was in the army when he got leave, he always went home to his parents. He said it was closer. He said it would be easier for him to find a job in Spartanburg. Our son was walking, being potty trained, and saying a lot of words and could make some short sentences. Everybody thought he was doing so well. He could say words plainly, and he had been shown so much love. I had taught him so many things. He would often want a hug because that's what he was used to getting at my parents' house. He was the first grandchild. He started getting spanked for every time he had an accident. One day I said something to Oscar about how well I thought the baby was doing and he slapped me right in front of his family. He told me to shut up. His grandmother would yell at him about spanking the baby and being mean to me. His other family encouraged it and told him, "You are right, you have to spank children." I found out that his parents fought and how his mother had stabbed his father so many times. His cousins told me that she bragged about having stabbed his dad everywhere except under the bottom of his feet. While in Spartanburg, I heard so many horror stories about the abuse on his mother's father side of the family. It was a way of life—getting drunk and fighting.

I felt stuck. After three months, he told me to write my dad and ask him to get the money in the bank and send all I had saved because we were going to Washington, D. C. because they were hiring there. I was glad to get to leave. I was tired of the smoking, drinking, and loud music. I wanted to get away from his family and didn't care where we went as long as it wasn't to Youngstown, Ohio, to live with his parents. I thought things would be better for us living alone in a new town, although by now I knew my marriage was never going to be as I was used to seeing at home. In fact, I had never seen people who called themselves Christians act like what I had seen so far or anybody act like what I had seen since I had gotten married. I had never seen my dad even raise his voice at Mom and hitting her was unthinkable. Dad had Mom to call and told her to ask me if everything was all right and I said yes. He said, "Your mom and I don't want you to stay with anybody if they aren't good to you. Remember what I told you that your Mom and I have done a good job raising all of you." I said, "Okay, Dad." He sent me the money and the address and telephone number of my Uncle Buck who lived in Washington D. C. and asked me to get in touch with him when I got there. He also asked me to call as soon as we got settled to let them know that we were all right. I know they were worried because they had called Uncle Buck and told them that we were coming and we would get in touch with him. Knowing my parents, they walked the floor and prayed and Dad would look for special scriptures when he was worried and Mom would write prayers on little pieces of paper. I know all of this was going on at home now more than ever.

PART III

WASHINGTON DC BECOMES HOME

Unhappiness Comes for a Lengthy Visit

The three of us left for Washington, D. C., and when we arrived we didn't call my uncle. Oscar said we would be all right. We got a paper and looked for vacant apartments. After hours, we saw an ad by a Christian woman looking for a Christian couple with no more than one child. We called her, and she said to come out to look at the place. It was in a nice neighborhood and the house was beautiful. We liked the place and moved in. We didn't have money to buy cigarettes and alcohol because the money was getting low. I was so happy and the landlady (Ann Chambers) kept the baby while we looked for a job every day. We came home and cooked and the baby could feed himself. I thought things were going well until one night I cooked some spinach and the baby ate everything except the spinach. He kept holding it in his jaw. Oscar kept saying, "Swallow that spinach." When we left the kitchen, he grabbed this belt and started hitting the baby, saying, "You don't show off on me." I asked him, "What did he do?" He said, "I told him to eat his spinach, and look, he is holding it in his jaw." I started crying more than the baby and told him that we were going home. He said, "Go ahead, but you aren't taking the baby." I told him that I would never leave the baby with him. The next day, he apologized and told me that he was sorry. He didn't look for a job that day and spent time with the baby. I went out to look for a job, and when I got back, the landlady told me what good care he had given the baby. I joined a church that following Sunday where the landlady attended. The baby and I would go to church every Sunday with her or we rode the bus. I had been taught to join a church as soon as you move to a new location because that's what the Baptist Covenant stated.

A Job—I Thought the Worst Was behind Us

The money was almost gone. I got a housekeeping job next door. I made enough to buy food, rent, and for the landlady to keep the baby while I worked. He started taking civil service exams. We had very little, but things were going well after the baby's last spanking over the spinach. I knew the worst was behind us. When Christmas came I made us a tree from green tissue paper. We bought things for the baby, and he asked for money to buy me something. He didn't get anything, but he was glad to see us happy. His family and my family also sent us gifts. During the holidays, the landlady's daughter, her boyfriend and grandson came over (Nancy, Clifton and Derrick). She and her boy friend drank and smoked. They asked us to join them. I said no thanks but we went down anyway and he joined them drinking and smoking. When they began to get drunk, they kept trying to get me to take a drink. I said no because the only time we had alcohol in our house was in the camphor bottle for headaches. I said to Oscar, "Let's go, the baby is getting sleepy." He said, "Go ahead," and we left. They went out and got Chinese food and he brought me some.

Oscar Gets a Job

His going out looking for a job turned into two or three times a week instead of every day. I continued working next door. He started taking care of the baby, and I didn't have to pay anyone to keep him anymore. One day someone stopped by who did construction work. I knew things were going to be better. We would have more money and would be able to move from the house where we were living. We both were excited. I thought this is the way it should be. We were where we should be, the man was supposed to take of his family. This is what my brothers had been taught. However, Dad would say I want my girls to be able to take care of themselves. Oscar got a job working construction, and he didn't seem to mind even though he had a degree and was at the top of his class in his field. Things started going bad after his first paycheck. He had money to buy alcohol and cigarettes. When Nancy and Clifton came over, they took turns buying alcohol and Chinese food. They would eat and drink for hours.

New Beginnings and Another Baby

I was expecting our second child. We had more money, but he was not spending it wisely. I had to stop working because it was getting too hard for me. One day an announcement from the post office in downtown Washington, D. C. came in the mail; it was regarding a job as postal clerk. Oscar was hired a few weeks before our first daughter (Voe) was born. She was so pretty and still is. He thought she was pretty also and would stare at her and kiss her. My son was happy to have a little sister. He would hug her, kiss her, and hold her hands. When she got a few months old, we went to church every Sunday. My husband was drinking too much and usually had a hangover on Sunday.

One day the landlady told him that she was going up on the rent because of the baby. He told me to start looking for another place to stay. I was so happy because the baby was young and I was staying home. She wasn't very nice to us because we were looking for another place to stay instead of paying her more money. He was working nights, and he told me that he would watch the children while I looked for another place to stay. I found a place in a house that had been turned into apartments. The apartment had to be cleaned before we could move in, which took about a week. There were two vacancies—one on first floor and one on second floor. We took the one on the first floor.

The Beginning of the Bells' Family Plan

My oldest brother had gotten out of the army, and he asked me if he could come and live with me until he found a job. I know I had to keep this promise to help each other. Oscar was told about it before we were married, and he was happy to have my brother stay with us. He got out right on time. By the time the landlord got our apartment ready, the apartment upstairs was perfect and ready also. We had a first cousin who had just graduated from college, and we all stayed together for about two or three days. They took the apartment upstairs and found jobs at St. Elizabeth Hospital in Washington D. C. They worked different shifts from my husband. Working at the post office was good as far as having enough money. We bought things for the apartment and for the children. Easter was coming up, and I bought an Easter basket for my son and things for them to wear to church. I kept imagining them being dressed very pretty and we would go to church. Oscar wanted some money to buy something, and I only had a few dollars left. He slapped me and started hitting me. My son started screaming, and a lady who lived in the apartment down in the basement came up to see what was going on. He kept right on hitting me. I took the things back and gave him the money. He left and came back with something prettier, but I looked too bad to go to church. He sat and stared into space off and on all the next day. He reported off sick from work the next day and didn't say a word for weeks. When I tried to talk to him, I got one-word answers, and I stopped trying to talk to him.

A Combination of Good and Bad for the Family

Now my son and daughter were old enough to go to nursery school. It was time for them to start playing with other children. We had enough money to get another apartment close to a school. We moved near J. C. Nall in the southeast of Washington D. C. My son loved it. I would take my daughter and volunteer some days at the school. I was soon asked to be a substitute teacher. My brother Dwight would bring me money every time he got paid to help us out because I had another brother named Will Oliver who would soon be getting out of the army. He knew what the family had talked about and we were trying to keep the plan we had made to help each other. Will Oliver moved in with me because I was expecting a baby and had two other small children. I was due soon with the new baby, and he wanted to be there to help me out when Oscar was working. He hadn't found a job yet, and the money he would be getting from unemployment would be a very big help. When Will's unemployment started, he gave me money every time he got a check, studied for civil service exams, and helped where he could.

After a short while, Will got a job working with our brother Dwight and first cousin Richard Hall at St. Elizabeth Hospital. Oscar was working at the post office, and the three of them studied for the post office exam and everyone passed with high scores. All three were hired and worked at the same post office with Oscar. During this time my husband became very unhappy about something. I was ready to have another daughter, and my oldest daughter was only a year and two months old. Everybody seemed happy. My brother Dwight and my cousin Richard lived together.

About two weeks before my second daughter, Sharolyn, was born, Oscar called me and told me that when he got home he wanted my brother out of the apartment. I asked him where he would go. He said, "I don't care." I also told him that he wanted to stay here until I had the baby so he could help me out. He repeated, "I want him gone." I called my uncle and told him what was happening and to ask Will to come live with him and don't let him know what was going on. I heard him trying to convince my uncle that he should stay there and help me with the babies because I would have two in diapers. After a while, I saw my brother get his things and leave. He looked so sad and I was sad and cried until Oscar got home. I asked him, "What did my brother do? Why did he have to leave?" He looked at me and kept walking. My brother wanted so badly to stay until I had the baby so he could help me with two babies. My parents were upset because he moved out before the baby came. I never told them why my brother had moved until forty-two years later.

Friends at the Post Office

Oscar had made friends at the post office and they would go out drinking after work. Sometimes he wouldn't get home until it was almost time to go to work. He gave himself enough time to take a bath and change clothes. One morning he brought his friends home and they sat around drinking until they woke up everybody. When they got ready to leave, he got ready to leave also. They were saying, "Man, aren't you going to stay home?" He said, "For what?" and he left with them. When he came back, he started hitting me. He threw me down on the floor and went to step on my stomach. I screamed, "Don't step on my stomach!" I avoided my brothers and cousin. I wouldn't answer the door. I didn't want them to see me because I knew they would have almost killed him. I told him that we needed counseling; we couldn't continue living like this. He told me that he didn't need counseling but I should go if it would make me feel better. I went and the counselor told me that he should come the next time. He didn't go and on the day Oscar was off, Father Merrow came to the house for a visit. It was in the evening, and he waited a few minutes for Oscar to come home so he could talk to both of us together. He didn't come home, and after he didn't for about a half hour, Father Merrow waited in the car, but he never came until much later. However, he did go with me the next time because he felt badly for missing Father Merrow. We had counseling for several months. We loved Father Merrow's company, and he always had something for us. He was a friend that we met at the corner drug store.

I Got Hired at the Federal Bureau of Investigation

One of his friends told him that the Federal Bureau of Investigation was hiring and his girlfriend had gotten hired. He told me that I should go apply. I applied and got hired, along with several others. (We eventually lost track of each other. Only one knew about my secret life of abuse.) I was able to work for approximately four years and got a promotion and never missed a raise as promised when I started working there. After three years had gone by I was expecting my third daughter, Wendolyn. I was working in the identification department where I had to stand or lean over on the counter where I was working. When I got too heavy on my feet, they transferred me to a sit-down job.

For some reason, the FBI was watching Oscar. I was called into the office and asked why my husband was coming home so late. I told them that he worked nights. At that time when they called me in, it was during the Christmas season and he was working a lot of overtime. They called me in again and shared a different story with me where the police had seen him. I was asked to resign because he was an embarrassment to the bureau. My reply was, "I haven't done anything. I am the one who works here, and I don't want to quit my job." Oscar resigned from the post office about three months before I went on maternity leave. Now he wasn't working and couldn't draw unemployment, so he took his money out of his retirement fund to last three or four months. I had had a C-section, and the doctor kept me off from work for eight weeks. He wanted me to stay off longer, but we needed the money. Oscar took care of me and the children and rushed out to look for a job some days without any success.

A Visit from My In-laws

His parents came down to visit us. They liked the apartment and were happy to see the children. He used almost all of the money from his retirement money to make things comfortable for them and to show them around. They had a good time and told us the next time it would be our turn to come visit. They were so proud of our accomplishments. What they didn't know was when they left the money left too. Things got really bad. There were days when we had oatmeal three times a day. We bought formula for the baby first. I tried to get an advance on my first check. I was denied. The person I talked to said no and remarked, "You are having a hard time?"

Back to Work for Me

I went back to work, and one day on my way home, I was praying that everybody would be out of the house. I came in the house and fell on my knees beside the bed and poured out my heart to God. When I got up, I went and set the table and went to the mailbox. There was a check in the mailbox from the electric company from where we had put a deposit down when we first moved in the apartment. It was supposed to be returned after six months if you paid your bill on time. They had forgotten to send it back at six months and it was in the box with interest. We ate well for about two weeks, along with some money from my brother and groceries from my Uncle Buck. About five months after his parents were down for a visit, I wrote them that I was the only one working and that he had been out of work since before they came to visit. They said they asked him if he was going to work. He said that he would be all right and they thought he was home because they were there and to show them around. I told them that I couldn't take the stress anymore. His mother told me to call him to the phone. When they asked him about it, he denied it and looked at me and he told them the truth. He told them that he was asked to resign. He didn't know why because he exceeded expectations on everything he did. I am sure he knew, but he refused to tell, or he may have been tired of the stress that was put on me by their inquiring as to his whereabouts. He said he never made lower than ninety-five on any of the tests at the post office. I believed that because he was a very smart person academically. I thought constantly about the times I would say, "I want a husband just like my dad," but I didn't want him to be a preacher. Dad stressed that it was his job to make sure the family got what they needed—love, food, shelter, and clothing. I wanted my husband to also be a good, God-fearing man who loved the Lord. Oscar had to get a job because the stress was making me ill. Had he showed love for God at this time, it may not have been so bad. We all agreed that he needed a job right then because we had four children who counted on us for their livelihood.

PART IV

MOVE TO YOUNGSTOWN, OHIO

Chapter V
Introduced to Another World

About a week later, we got his clothes cleaned and all packed. He went to Youngstown, Ohio, and got a job a week later working as a group leader for Associated Neighborhood Centers. It was in his field. His major was sociology with a minor in English. He was a very good social worker and helped a lot of youth find their first jobs. He also counseled families and made a difference. After he had worked for four months, he asked me to come up for a visit. I went for a visit because my sister Eleanor had come up to go to school and to stay with us. He came home three times before we went down, but he would call me and the children almost two or three times a week. He never sent a penny home for over a year to help with anything. He asked for a Christmas list for the children, and he came home with a footlocker filled with toys and clothes for the children and some of the best cologne for me. We had a great Christmas. We hated to see him leave. I was sad, and so were the children.

A year had passed, and in August of 1968, he had saved up enough money to move us to Youngstown, Ohio. We stayed with his parents for about three days while a friend of theirs got a house ready for us to move in. I heard his mother telling someone on the phone that she was surprised he moved us there and when he started talking about bringing us to where he was she didn't think anything about it. She said, "She," meaning me, "didn't want him around when he wasn't working, and I am surprised he went back for them." When he got home that day from work she brought out a picture of his high school girlfriend, and both of them would comment. I was there, and they talked as if I wasn't. They talked about some of the funny things she had done. He was still carrying her picture in his wallet. When he went to bed I took it out of his wallet, and he didn't miss it for a long time, so evidentially he didn't ever look at it. I know my parents never, ever would have done something like this! How awful, I thought, to do this to me. I didn't have anybody to talk to but God. I thought, *What an awful mother-in-law—no empathy for me!*

Our Own House

Once we had settled in our house, we checked out the neighborhood. We found a church and the school that the children would be attending. He took the two older children to school on the first day and I stayed at home with the two youngest children. He met the principal and the children's teachers. He was excited and impressed with the school and told me when the first PTA meeting was going to be and that the president lived on the next street. When the children left for school every morning, I didn't pray out loud as my mother did. I prayed silently and told them that it was a mean world out there and I wanted them to go out and make good choices. I would say over and over, "I am going to be a good mother. I know I can be, and I love being a mother."

It was a very nice neighborhood, and this was the first time I had heard of the welcome wagon. A lady stopped by with all kinds of coupons, samples, and other things that we could use. It seemed as if we were getting off to a good start. We also met some young couples that would visit and we would visit them. We had more children than the other couples so I thought it was best if they came to our house because we didn't have transportation. They were from different backgrounds than I was or developed it after leaving home, as some young folks do. I hadn't seen women drinking and smoking before. To be truthful, I had seen very few men smoking. Among Christians, this was a sin and if asked, God would deliver you. We came to really love each other and our children did also.

During these first few months, sometimes his mother would pick him up from work. There were times when he pretended that he was mad with me about something and he would spend the night at his parent's house. It usually happened on a Friday and they would go to a bar. When his mother drove him home the next day, both of them came in laughing as if nothing had happened. Occasionally, you could smell the alcohol. This went on for six months. She died of a heart attack six months to the day after we had moved to Youngstown, Ohio. The family was saddened, and we cried off and on for months and my faith in God got me through this awful time in our lives. He was saddened for a long time and would hug her picture and cry. I felt so bad for him and soon found out that he used this to manipulate me.

Using His Mom's Death to Manipulate

Sometimes he would be sitting downstairs late at night and I would hear him sobbing out loud and I would go to see what was wrong. He would be sitting there with her picture in his hand and sobbing. Occasionally he would say, "I need a drink. Let's go to SO SOS or another bar." I would go with him and sit while he drank and listened to music and laughed with the guys. He would always introduce me to the people who came over, or he would call someone he knew and say, "Come over and meet my wife." This way he got a free drink because they would always ask, "What is she drinking?" He would tell them something, and a drink was sent over. I was so miserable because this was something that I didn't want to do. I was being a loving, devoted wife who wanted to see her husband through these difficult times. If he needed someone to talk to I wanted to be there for him. I was going to set an example for the drinkers and just sit there and drink water or ginger ale. One night one of his friends stopped over and asked him what I was drinking and I said water. He took my hand and I thought he was being compassionate and I got this hard squeeze. When the guys found out I was drinking water or ginger ale, one said, "Man, why do you make your wife come here and she doesn't drink?" He started doing his traditional chin rubbing that he usually did when he was drinking. He stopped asking me to go unless we were with another couple, and if she drank, I would sit and talk to her. During this awful time when we were grieving profusely, he still managed to be mean and get his digs in. I ignored them and catered to his every desire.

Self Inventory and Counseling

It was past time for me to take inventory of my life, so I set some goals and visualized what it would be like for the children if I didn't change the course I was on. This is not the kind of atmosphere I was brought up in, and I wasn't going to bring our children up in this kind of atmosphere. I didn't want this kind of life and wanted something better for myself and for my children. God was always first in our life and in our house. I set goals for myself and was determined to get a job and go back to school. I told him that we needed to talk. I poured out everything I had been thinking. He listened as I gave my say, "I don't appreciate going to bars sitting with you," and by this time I was on the verge of screaming. "I hate when you and your friends try to get me to take a drink. I was going to join a church and get a job. The children will continue to go to church and Sunday school to the church at the end of our block where they can walk. We have to get counseling." For once I thought he was hearing me and was going to change. We got counseling bi-weekly for several months by a psychologist. We found out that the psychologist and his wife were having problems also. We had joint sessions, and then she and I had sessions together and the two of them together. Things were better for about eleven months after the sessions stopped and the silent treatments started again.

My First Job in Youngstown, Ohio

I got a job working at Union National Bank as the first Negro downstairs in the consumer loans department as a teller. Things went well for me there. I learned some other jobs and was asked to fill in when some of the other staff was on vacation. Mr. Redmond was the vice president and showed a lot of confidence in me. I worked there for one year and a few days. We didn't have a car, and both of us rode the bus to and from work. Sometimes he would get a ride home with friends and I would too. The opportunity came for me to get a better job. An opening came available at Clarence Robinson Day Care for a supervisor. I hated to leave the bank, but the job paid more money, and it was in walking distance from home. I also saw so much potential in having a job like this and I had experienced working and teaching children at church and from helping my great-grandmother at her school.

Clarence Robinson Day Care Center

I began working at the center, and the staff and I got off to a good start, but they didn't hesitate to remind me of what the previous supervisor had done. Previously, it had been more or less a play school. I turned it into a learning school and changed the atmosphere to demonstrate the same. An opportunity came available for me to go back to school. Some of the staff wanted to get more education, and I wanted them to do so too. I gave them workshops on alternative teaching methods, and they attended other training that became available. If the traditional way of doing things didn't work, we brainstormed and sought alternative methods for reaching the children. In the class that I was taking during this time at Youngstown, State University, I shared some new teaching ideas that my staff and I had discovered, and the instructor, who was an elementary school principal, said that he was going to share the ideas with his teachers, and he did. I changed the entire make-up of the school at Clarence Robinson Center. The parents were satisfied and raved about the things we were doing. As supervisor, the teachers and I started a parent-teacher group and the school started getting visits from teachers of other day care centers to observe the things we were doing. Oscar began criticizing in some small way regardless of how outstanding the situation turned out. The things I was doing made both of us look good. I went to the library and checked out books, waited impatiently for the weekend newspaper to read the section entitled "Book Review," attended workshops and seminars, had my own workshops, and brought other teachers to Clarence Robinson Center Day Care. I managed to get several certificates in different areas of early childhood education, and I read at least three or four books a week, depending on the size. To further help the agency and myself, I filled out an application for a federal government grant so we could expand the food program for some free meals for the students. I got enough meals for breakfast, lunch, and an evening snack. The agency was on the move, and we got federal attention.

I was becoming known and began to look at my wardrobe. I dressed very modestly. I wanted to look better for church and wanted to look successful for work. This is when I joined a fabric club and my sewing skills became useful. I got some good bargains on fabric, and I hadn't forgotten how to sew with or without a pattern. The girls got five new outfits, one for each day for the first week of school. My son got his five outfits from the store, and I would make him a vest or bow tie to wear occasionally. Since things were going well at work and at home, I thought I would make something for myself. A sewing club was started at work, and four of us got new sewing machines. We diligently assisted each other with individual projects. This was really a treat for me. I had an outfit for each work day, but I only had two outfits for church. I had a plain black dress and a beige suit. Having only two outfits for church didn't bother me at all. With the black dress that had a round neckline, I wore jewelry with it one Sunday, a scarf another, and a detachable collar one Sunday. With the beige suit, it was made high enough to wear a blouse under it one Sunday and with a broach or something else on another Sunday. Oscar became very unhappy and started ignoring my friends to the point that he wouldn't speak to them. Eventually his relationship with my friends broke up and I couldn't go to their house and they felt uncomfortable coming to mine. He criticized the clothes I was wearing. I didn't stop, and as time went by and I continued to get compliments, he stopped criticizing and didn't say anything. This was fine with me. I learned to make curtains, draperies, matching bed spreads, and a tablecloth with matching napkins. He never said anything to me, but I heard him tell his cousins and friends that I could make anything. He would tell them about the things I had made or was making for the house. I had finally made him proud and was on the right track and things would be better and he would stop criticizing the things I did, I thought.

An Outing That Caused Life-threatening Consequences

A few months later, a cousin of Oscar's (Benny) asked us to join her and boyfriend on an outing. I had agreed to go out with him sometime and I did. I didn't sit quietly as I had always done. They thought I was funny, and we laughed. Suddenly I felt this kick under the table and this awful pinch. I kept quiet for a while and started getting sleepy and closed my eyes and I felt this hard pinch again. I suggested that we call it a night. Of course, I was the only one ready. I prayed to God and asked Him to give me the courage to walk out and get me a cab. The next time I got a pinch I got up and left. I knew the agreement we had made was over. I went in the basement and hid in the bathroom. I had my clothes on just sitting with the lid down. I fell asleep, and I didn't hear him come down the stairs. He found me and jerked back the plastic door, grabbed me by the hair, and drug me all over the basement floor, beating me. I tried to fight back because we had had a serious conversation about this kind of behavior. As he was hitting me, he told me that I embarrassed him by falling asleep and getting up and leaving. I started screaming and told him that he should leave me at home. I woke the children and my sister up. The children came running downstairs, saying, "Mommy, Mommy!" A whole plug of hair was missing. One eye was swollen shut, and the other side of my face was sagging. The children thought I was doing things to make him the way he was. When I cried, my son would wipe my eyes while the girls looked on and said, "Mommy, next time, don't do anything to make him mad." I told them that Mommy didn't do anything. Now I believe this was my major signal to leave. My thoughts were the next time he will accidentally kill you. This time he pleaded and begged for forgiveness. He cried for the first time and told me how sorry he was. I forgave him but did not forgive myself for putting up with this kind of life. This time, the same as sometimes before, it left me feeling guilty because he had a way of making me feel that it was my fault, that I contributed to or solicited this horrible behavior.

A New Trend

He started a new trend. We didn't have a car, I walked to the grocery store, and he would always send Oscar III with me. Even though I thought he was too young to walk these long distances, he sent him anyway. We would get a taxi back. One day just as I was leaving the grocery store. I saw a lady that I had met at the PTA meeting, and she gave us a ride home. He wouldn't come out to help bring the groceries in the house. I asked him to come help me so I wouldn't have to make so many trips. He looked at me and said, "Bring them in your damn self." When I had brought the last bag in the house, he told me, "Don't you ever let a man drive you up in front of my house." I asked, "What man?" He said, "I saw him and he didn't help you bring the groceries in because he didn't want me to see him." I was speechless and told him that was a lady that I had met at a PTA meeting. He sat and stared rubbing his right hand across his chin, as he would usually do when he was thinking about something.

For some reason he must have felt awful because he took me out to dinner and there was no drinking, which created false hope. We came home at a reasonable time and listened to some music. He liked jazz and the blues and most of the hits in the '60s. I liked gospel and some of the jazz hits. The blues sounded too sad for me. We played both. It was near Valentine's Day, and I got this huge box of candy and about four or five cards. He even had enough money to buy me a new dress. The somewhat good days went on for about two years or a little longer. He often told me how much he loved me. The drinking wasn't as bad as it had been at times before. I thought he was really making an effort to be different. I became creative and tried to think of things that would make me a better person. I read my Bible more, prayed, and thought about going to Al-Anon to help me cope with the drinking. I needed a car to get to Al-Anon, and things were looking better for me.

Our First Car

I had saved some money and asked Oscar to come with me to see if we could get a car. He refused and told me to go ahead. I asked my brother Clarence to go with me, and he did after trying to get Oscar to go. We went to a Chevy dealer and were told to come back the next day to get the car. I asked Oscar to go to driving school with me so we could learn to drive. He didn't want to go. He said that he already knew how to drive but that he never got his license after he got out of the army because we couldn't afford a car. I learned to drive anyway. There were many advantages to having a car. We could go when we were ready without someone driving us or getting a cab, and we could be alone with just our children. I got the car before I learned to drive. Having the car first was a big motivator and I could hardly wait to learn to drive and take the driving test. Every thing went well and I got my driver's license. It was a long time before Oscar would ride with me but it didn't stop me and the children from riding together.

Al-Anon

I started attending Al-Anon and tried to get Oscar to go to Alcoholics Anonymous but was unable to do so. I managed to go on with my life by trying to ignore his drinking as long as it didn't turn ugly the best I could. Weekly, I liked seeing the other women. Some mates were alcoholics only and some were also abusive. The sad thing was (in the group where I attended) no one seemed to be getting away from these awful situations. It was some relief to see that I was not alone by living with an alcoholic. Some mates had attended Al-Anon for years and some spouses were sober and some weren't. After some time had passed, I felt that the abuse was over and tried not to think about it changing, although we had had these honeymoon periods many times before. However, this time I was going to make my marriage work because God had finally answered my prayers. I knew God had finally answered, I knew it, and the times before were crosses I had to bear! I told myself that God bore a cross and this was mine. I knew He was going to change him because this time I was doing something to help myself. I would be a better person by going to Al-Anon. The honeymoon periods before had ended abruptly, but this time it would be different!

More time than ever before had gone past, and one day my husband's bad habits started again. I was devastated. He had started drinking again and rarely came straight home from work. Although he drank heavily, he could always manage to get up and go to work. He was smart, suggesting ideas that were accepted, expanding new programs, and more people got hired to do these additional jobs. When the executive director's job of Associated Neighborhood Centers, which consisted of five community centers on different sides of town, came available, Oscar was asked by the personnel committee of the board of directors to be the first Negro executive director for these five centers. He was an outstanding worker, and people in each community really liked him and supported him in major endeavors he undertook.

PART V

"I CAN DO ALL THINGS THROUGH CHRIST WHICH STRENGTHENS ME" (Philippians. 4:13, KJV).

Chapter VI
A Church Home

Although I was a member of a church, Oscar found a church that he liked and once I visited, I liked it too. It was a church home, at last, where the family could worship together. We went to church for months, and I kept asking Oscar to join Antioch Baptist Church since we both liked it and the children had made friends also. On the second Sunday in September of that year, 1970, we joined the church, and I knew for sure this undertaking was going to make a vast, if not total, difference from the way things had been going on in our marriage—worshiping together, studying for Sunday school together, and planning activities for the youth department. The change that I was praying for years was finally here. Through prayer and letting my light shine where people could see the fruit of Christianity shining through, I knew this would make a difference. I became stronger in the Lord and my daily sayings throughout the day were, "I can do all things through Christ which strengthens me," and please, Lord, "Create in me a good heart and renew the right spirit in me." I wanted to be a virtuous woman as described in Proverbs 31:10–31. I was far, far, far from perfect when I compared myself to Jesus Christ, but I was equal and much better than some of the women I knew and associated with. When Oscar wanted to be very nasty and mean, he would say, "I want a virtuous woman as a wife," as if I wasn't and moments later he would say, "I love you and always will." He didn't know, or maybe he did, that I was trying with every fiber of my body to be one. Another time when he wanted to be nasty, he and his friend drank too much to go home and his friend's wife called me and told me that her husband had drunk too much to drive Oscar home and they were going to let him sleep there and bring him home the next morning. I apologized and thanked them. When he woke up his friend's wife told him that she had called me and told me where he was and he had to get home. He became angry and told her that she should mind her own business. He thought I didn't worry enough. "I wanted her to be worried."

He wanted a virtuous wife, but he was nothing like the husband I dreamed of having. Proverbs describes a virtuous woman. I will take the time to put the description right here so you won't have to get your Bible in order to read it. I wasn't concerned about how other people saw me or marveled over me. I wanted my husband to see me and think I was someone special.

A Virtuous Woman Described

Proverbs 31:10–31 (KJV)

Who can find a virtuous woman? for her price is far above rubies.
The heart of her husband doth safely trust in her, so that he shall have no need of spoil. She will do him good and not evil all the days of her life.
She seeketh wool, and flax, and worketh willing with her hands.
She is like the merchants' ships; she bringeth her food from afar.
She riseth also while it is yet night, and giveth meat to her household, and a portion to her maidens.
She considereth a field, and buyeth it; with the fruit of her hands she planeth a vineyard. She girdeth her loins with strength, and strengtheneth her arms.
She perceiveth that her merchandise is good: her candle goeth not out by night.
She layeth her hands to the spindle, and her hands hold the distaff.
She stretcheth out her hand to the poor: yea, she reachest forth her hands to the needy. She is not afraid of the snow for her household: for all her household are clothed with scarlet.
She maketh herself coverings of tapestry; her clothing is silk and purple.
Her husband is known in the gates, when he sitteth among the elders of the land.
She maketh fine linen, and selleth it; and delivereth girdles unto the merchants.
Strength and honour are her clothing; and she shall rejoice in time to come.
She openeth her mouth with wisdom; and in her tongue is the law of kindness.
She looketh well to the ways of her household, and eateth not the bread of idleness.

Her children arise up, and call her blessed; her husband *also,* and he praiseth her.
Many daughters have done virtuously, but thou excellest them all.
Favour is deceitful, and beauty is vain: but a woman that feareth the Lord, she shall be praised.
Give her of the fruit of her hands; and let her own works praise her in the gates.

Continued Visible Growth

Several people from church and work noticed my continued growth in the Lord except the person I wanted most to notice—Oscar. We went to Sunday school and church every Sunday. He taught Sunday school, and I did too. Many times I was told by other women that they were grooming their daughters to be just like me. I would say thank you and say silently, "Lord, I sure hope not. If they only knew about the load I am carrying.

When election for new officers came up, I was voted youth director unanimously. The pastor asked some people to work with me as advisors and they accepted. Our children participated in the youth department, and one sang in the youth choir. After two years, my pastor, Reverend Alfred Ward, started looking at Oscar for a deacon. Pastor Ward soon made him a deacon, and I became a deaconess. We were a big help to the pastor. People at church and the community thought we were the perfect family because the children always had plenty of clothes, toys, and food to eat and all the children had the same last name. One day my son came home from little league football and asked me, "Why do all of us have the same last name but some of my friends' sisters and brothers have different last names?" I explained to him it was because all of them had the same father. He must have understood because he didn't continue the conversation. When I told my husband, he laughed and thought it was funny.

I loved Antioch Baptist Church, which had a congregation of approximately 325 people or less. Aside from being the youth director, I became chairperson of the deaconess ministry. God truly had His hands on me. I was somewhat of a new member when I became chairperson. The pastor was criticized because my husband and I were not from the Store Front Church on West Federal Street and some members felt that he was allowing us to do too many things. The store front people thought they should have been the only ones to have any major roles in church. I started the first preschool Sunday school class. The advisors and I started an outing for the youth on the third Sunday evening of each month. It was well attended, even though we were a small church. At some of our functions, we would have over a hundred children. A group of women and I later started a health and safety ministry. I sought donations for the church and became the chairperson of the pastor's anniversary committee, which lasted twenty-six years. There were some people I could count on year after year—Ann Carter, Audrey Harris, Deacon Ernest James, Robert Jennings, Deacon and Mrs. John Livas, Deacon Oscar Murphy Jr., John Perdue, Deacon and Mrs. Andrew Rushing, Samuel and Arlene Overton, Lillie Woodberry, Ruth Adams, and the late Dottie Breedlove. When women were put on the trustee ministry, I was one of the first women. Outside leaders came to our church and did workshops on various topics, and the church embraced the idea. There were certain people in church who I talked to the pastor about honoring because of the things that I saw they had done and was led by God to move on. The events were successful. I have many success stories from this church. I don't want to sound as if I am bragging, but I saw it as a blessing—our offerings were much higher than any other members'. When we joined, the men were paying $2.50 on Sunday and the women were paying $1.50 per Sunday. Being a preacher's kid, I knew what it took to run a church and I didn't mind giving because I knew from experience God would bring it back three-fold. I had too many unexplained good things to happen that could only be contributed to God showing favor than to fall short with giving.

The Murphy's House Was the Place to Go

We moved to another house right down the street from where we were living. It was for sale, and we purchased it. There were several children in our neighborhood, and they all came to our house. I kept my children at home when they weren't in school or at church. If the other children wanted to play with them, our house is where they came to play. Some loved to come to our house and would go immediately to the refrigerator and asked for something to eat. Often when they finished eating, some wanted to watch television. One kid asked me if she could make a sandwich as soon as she came through the door. We couldn't grow any grass in our yard until the last child was in the tenth grade. One daughter was a cheerleader and on the dance line at school. I couldn't keep carpet long in the dining room and living room because they practiced their cheers there after we pushed the furniture back. There was a hole between the living room and dining room where their heels landed in the same place on the floor and when they did their splits. I didn't care; they weren't going to stay children always.

My daughters also participated in debutante balls. They were referred to as the Cinderella ball. My middle daughter was first runner up one year, and the youngest daughter was crowned Miss Cinderella. The oldest daughter supported her sisters and didn't care to compete in the balls. She went to charm school and learned to play the flute. Along with her sisters, they successfully participated in many other activities. One of their favorites was getting an acting role in a play and another was being given leadership roles in the neighborhood, school, and church. My son started his own band at an early age, played little league football, and learned to play several instruments.

There were three children who loved being at our house so much, they would stay for days and always had a legitimate reason not to go home. They would go home, get clothes, and come right back for a couple of days. One parent never came to meet us or see where her daughter was staying. I would call her mother and invite her over, but she too always had a reason not to come. We were going out of town and

I called her to pick her up and she drove up and blew the horn before I could get to the door to go out to meet her. If it seems as if I was being abused by parents also. I thought so too. Out of approximately thirty-two children who frequented our house, I haven't heard of any ever being in jail or any kind of trouble.

If my children wanted to go some place, I took them and volunteered as a chaperone. When some of the parents found out that I was dropping mine off and picking them up, they began dropping their children off at my house for me to take them. I called them and asked them to take turns with me. One parent told me, "You are going anyway, so why don't you continue because I have to do something at that time." No one wanted to take turns and one was a stay-at-home mom and I was working. One parent said she would take them if I picked them up. It was all right, because at least I was getting some help.

All four of our children seemed happy; the children were doing well in school, Sharolyn was making the straight-A honor roll, and the others were making the A and B honor roll and participating in extracurricular activities at school and church. The girls continued with dance lessons, modeling, piano lessons, flute lessons, the debate team, and track. Oscar III expanded his skills in the music world. His band received more and more opportunities for playing for different engagements. They did well throughout the city. When recital time came, Oscar and I both were there to see and clap for the children. We would take other children to see the recitals also if they were over and wanted to go. Afterward we always stayed for refreshments and fellowshipped with the other parents, which was all right. Another parent didn't take a turn with transportation but she helped me with gas money. Rather than help with the responsibility, another parent kept her children home sometimes and sneaked them in at other times and she could drive.

I didn't leave the other children much choice other than coming to our house because they wanted to play with our children. The reason my children were kept at home was because I didn't know what was going on in other homes. My mother would say the same thing when we were growing up. They weren't allowed to copy off other children as far as doing things we were uncomfortable with them doing. If they came home and said that another parent had let their child-do something that didn't meet our approval, they were told no, you be the pace setter. Let them copy off you. Stephen Covey would have called that being proactive. I insisted that they be the leader and let the others react to what they were doing. I was going to be a good mom. I had seen a good mom and dad. I kept telling myself that God was with me and must have answered my prayers. Oscar would drink every now and then on weekends. I was not totally relaxed because I kept thinking the abuse might come back without notice. True enough, when I came home one afternoon my clothes had been thrown from the second-story window in the driveway for being a little late coming home from work, and he didn't wait to ask why. He had created his own reason that was outrageous.

Satan Raises His Head

The church on the corner from our house was honoring their pastor, Reverend Elizabeth Powell. I told Oscar that we should go because of how the church had benefited us. They had great activities for the youth, and our children were always asked to participate. He didn't want to go. To show my appreciation, I purchased a ticket to go to the banquet. I needed a dress to wear and I couldn't go shopping through the week so I asked my next-door neighbor, Naomi Carr, to come with me on Saturday. We went shopping because she was going too and it took us hours to find something to wear. We got the bus and came home, and when I came through the door, he came out and I didn't see him until he hit me right over my left ear and burst my ear drum. I was in so much pain; he called one of his friends to drive us to the doctor. The family doctor looked at it and told me to go to an ear, nose, and throat specialist. When we got there, the doctor looked in the ear. He said, "It is swollen and red as if it was going to burst." The doctor and his nurse went into the outer room and were whispering about something. When he came back in he told me that I had been hit with an open hand and asked who did it. I made up some kind of story. He didn't push it. He said, "I am going to put something in there that will dissolve and fill the hole in, but you will always have a faint roaring in your ear. However, you will get used to it." We never talked about it again after I told him that the doctor knew what had happened. He dropped his head and didn't say anything.

A Major Step up for the Agency

In the early 1970s when Richard Nixon was president, through a grant, there was a program called Model Cities. I was the person who furnished the information for the Youngstown Early Childhood Education portion of the grant. Minnie Searcy was one of the top leaders in the total program. We became friends, and she gave me this opportunity. I had gotten Associated Neighborhood Center Day Care at Clarence Robinson Center upgraded, and it was also one of the target schools for some grant money. The other one was on the east side of the city. When my portion of the grant was finished, people with other interest soon finished their portions. The grant was submitted as one huge grant. We got every penny we asked for—$1.3 million. I was so happy and excited about the success. Even though another center on the east side of town that got some of the funds was not under our umbrella—Associated Neighborhood Centers—I was also elevated over that day care center. The attendance grew, and within three years there were four full-capacity day care centers and one nursery school with over ninety employees. I became the principal/administrator over all of them.

For this kind of achievement, this time, Oscar had to notice all the good things that I was doing. Instead of bringing someone in when a teacher was absent, I filled in myself to save money. I trained my teachers. We tried several programs that were successful, even Montessori. We had a speech instructor for the children at Clarence Robinson Center, the center where I started in the agency, and McGuffey Center. One of my aids could speak Spanish, and she taught some Spanish. Our class rooms at all the schools were always very pretty, with things to produce a learning environment. The soon-to-be Kindergarten-age children were excelling and passed the test for school. Some went to the first grade. I had the children of most of the professional families in the city. Day care centers from all over the city and surrounding areas came to visit the centers where I was the administrator. I was asked to come to two of the wealthiest area high schools—Canfield, Ohio, and Poland, Ohio—to talk to the students who were interested in early childhood education as a vocation. I shared with them the rewards for choosing this field as a major. We also talked about the need for the best teachers in early childhood education. The reason given was that this is where lasting learning begins, and children remember a huge percentage of what they learn during this time in life. I took some of the papers and crafts that the students had done, and they were amazed. My staff, family, and friends were so happy. Some of my parents told me and my staff that teachers looked forward to the students from our school because they knew our children would be fluent in the things that children should know at ages five and six. When my husband heard about me visiting these two schools, he wanted to know why I picked these two schools. I told him that I didn't, they selected me. He acted excited for a while and soon began his criticisms again. This could have been different, or you spent too much on that. It pushed me to work harder and harder, which was never enough. All I wanted was a comment or approval from him. I enjoyed the comments from my staff, parents, and other schools not under our umbrella. My church family heard about the achievements and my pastor, Reverend Alfred Ward, was happy that we were members of his church. My husband asked him to be on the board of directors. He accepted and would sometimes mention on Sunday about things some of the members were doing and asked the church members to support them.

We continued to go to church every Sunday. Oscar was drinking Friday and Saturday nights and managed to go to church on Sunday. He became the financial secretary at church. He was a very, very good one. In fact, he was the best they ever had. He started recording things that the members didn't know about. He recorded everything, and they loved his bookkeeping. Everybody seemed happy except me. I knew the other deacons and the pastor could smell the alcohol on him and would soon say something to him. By him being the financial secretary, there were some close-ups. I was really hurting, and I wanted someone to notice. I would say, "They have to know. Can't they see how unhappy I am? How long can I keep this up, Lord? I must be handling this too well, and I am going to stop smiling so much. They have to smell the alcohol!" Sometimes in Church I would be about to burst. How am I going to make it? How long will I be able to keep up this front? I would ask God to help me hold on a little longer. We would be going home soon. He would go straight out the door most of the time, and if some of the members would ask me something and he thought I was taking too long to come out, one time he ran back in and stuck his finger in my face and said, "I am tired of waiting for you." When I got to the car, I told him, "Don't you ever, ever do that again," and he didn't. When we got home he acted as if nothing ever happened and started talking about work over dinner.

Work was going well. The board of directors noticed all the great things that were happening at our schools and raved about them. Not only did I and the staff achieve things for the agency, but I also achieved some goals for myself. I was in school again taking one class at a time. My name was listed in Who's Who among American Colleges and Universities. I wrote a fifty-five typed page paper entitled, "The Struggles of Christian Women in the Church," and my instructor said it was some of the best work he had seen at Youngstown State University since he had been there. I was the first Black (we had changed from Negro) to become vice president of the Ohio Day Care Association. When the president resigned, I served as the president for a short time, although the day care centers all over the state wanted me to keep the job because we were having more training for the teachers and more schools became state and federally certified. This allowed them the opportunity to apply for state and federal funds. I knew I wouldn't be able to travel as much as the job demanded, so I stayed until someone was appointed. Some of my other accomplishments were that I served as the first early childhood education coordinator for Model Cities Day Care Centers. I was the first coordinator of United Way-funded day care centers. The criticism from Oscar continued, and I had come to a very dangerous zone. Instead of making my own decisions that were working so well for me, I started getting his approval on everything I did. I would present it to him, and 90 percent of the time he didn't comment, but had I gone ahead and done it without his approval, I would have been criticized.

One day I told him that since we had a car and I was over all of the agency schools and one other, I wanted to visit all the schools at least once a week. He told me to use the school van and have the bus driver take me around. That didn't work because the bus driver had other duties. I had an office that I used at each building, but he thought it would be best if I worked out of the headquarters, which was at the school on Lexington Avenue on the north side where his office was located. I didn't move right away. One day when I left the office to visit Hansen Center's school, I signed out when I left and the train caught me. He had called me twice before I got to the school. He was furious if I didn't get there by the time he thought I should been there. When I walked in, the director told me that he had called twice and to call him right away. I called him and he said, "Bitch, where have you been? Why don't you quit before I fire you?" I said the train caught me and I had to wait. He said, "My mamma didn't raise a fool," and slammed the phone down. When he got home late that night, I told him that when my children grew up I was not going to keep putting up with his mess. He looked at me as if I was mess and said, "F--- you, you can leave now if you want to." I never forgot that statement. I kept silent and didn't say a word to him for a long time. It was my turn this time to start the silence.

We had gotten to the place where we could take out-of-town vacations near and far, even though I was the only driver. If we went on long trips, we would stop a lot and stay overnight in a hotel. When we sat down for meals, the children were allowed to order whatever they wanted to eat. Whatever city we were in, we usually took a city tour to see the historic places. We went somewhere special every summer. Even though I would tire from doing all the driving, I enjoyed the fun times we had together.

I complained about how tired I would be after vacation, when I would have to go back to work. Oscar finally started driving. We went out for a few practice drives, and he went to take the written test and the road test and got his driver's license. I was happy because I didn't want all the responsibility of driving on vacations, driving him and the children to meetings, plus the other things I had to do.

Office Relocated—Something Good Happened?

My office was relocated in the same building as my husband's. If he was angry about something at home, he took it out on me at work. One day I was having a conference with one of the teachers and he came bursting in and asked for something and told me he wanted it right then. I got it for him. A few minutes later one of my parents told me that General Motors was hiring for a second shift and they had some good jobs. She further stated that her kid's teacher told her to stop in and let me know that she might be a little late some evenings but she would pay the additional cost. The wheels started turning—this was my time to get away. I got an application and got hired as a mig-welder. I didn't care how hard the work would be, I could adjust. I would make more money, finish school, and be able to make it for myself and the children. When I got off from work, I had to go by to pick him up because we didn't have a second car. I was so tired, plus I had to go home and cook dinner. Most time both of us helped the children with their home work.

One day the husband of one of my former employees, Walter Randolph, saw me mig-welding about two weeks after I started working, came over, took me by the arm, and told my supervisor to put someone in my place because he was taking me to personnel. (I was very proud of my welds. They were almost perfect. My job was to put two welds on the inner part of the section that held the tire rod. I put two welds there, one on each side of the opening. I would stand back and smile at how good I thought they looked.) When we got to personnel, he was still holding my shoulder. He told the personnel director that I had been a teacher, principal and an administrator and to please give me a job. He did, but my supervisor told me to stay on the job until he got someone else. He put me on another job until I completed ninety days. He told me that salaried employees were likely to get laid off before hourly employees and that way I could come back to the line. It didn't seem as if the ninety days would never get there. My right hand still shows the signs of squeezing the welding gun and also my right shoulder. I didn't care; I got some relief from Oscar. After the ninety days were over, I began working in scheduling and car distribution. The moves continue later in my story.

What an Imagination

I was the church clerk, and when I went to the church to do the bulletins for Sunday worship and for other programs, if it took longer than he thought it should, he always had something that he had made up when I got home. If the children's teachers stopped by he would say what he was thinking and go upstairs and wouldn't come back down. If they were couples, it didn't matter. Family could be visiting, and he would be nasty and make some remark about something I was supposed to have been doing. Sometimes it would be so ugly the visitors would stare at each other. One weekend my nieces from Dayton, Ohio was visiting—Yvette and Annette. After I fed the children, I went to the church to do the bulletins, and when I got there the old typewriter was really gone. I was not the only one who used it, and I called home to let everybody know that it was going to take longer than I thought because the person who used it last didn't notify anyone to get it fixed. I couldn't get it to work. I called the center director for Clarence Robinson Center and asked him if I could use the typewriter to do some typing. He said it was all right and came to unlock the door so I could get in the office. When I finished typing the bulletins, I didn't take time to fold them; I took them home so the children could help me fold them. As soon as I walked in the door, the children came to greet me and we folded the bulletins. I walked upstairs and my little niece was holding my hand. He came running out of the bedroom and hit me right in front of her. She started screaming and swinging her purse and called the other children at the top of her voice, "Come on you all." He went back in the room. My niece didn't go far; she was standing there swinging her little purse. When I began to think the worst was over, he came running out again and she started swinging her purse and calling the other children. He went back to the bed and she calmed them down by telling them that he went back to bed and everything was all right. It didn't matter to him that visitors were in the house.

I tried to do everything perfect to keep him happy. It didn't work. He always made up these imaginary things that I was doing. I was determined I was going to get it right. The silent periods got longer and longer. The arm twisting became more frequent. He started coming home later and later after work. Sometimes he would be gone for days. We kept going to church on Sunday and taking the kids. We ate out often as if we were the perfect family. Some people thought we were the perfect family. They didn't know how bad we were hurting, especially me. I continued the tradition Mom had started—having the big sit-down dinner on Sunday with the long grace. When we finished and did the dishes, the children and I would go and get in the bed and D'Vorolyn (Voe) would go ahead because she liked selecting movie, and this became her job after Sunday dinner. Very seldom would Oscar join us for the movie. He liked reading the paper and he would read it from cover to cover during this time.

The imagination became more and more gruesome. The name-calling was intense. He followed me, and at first I wondered how he was getting home right behind me. My middle daughter, Sharolyn, said, "Mom, he must be following you." I filed for a divorce. It came out in the paper. Everybody except me must have read that section in the paper. When I got to church the Sunday after the announcement was in the paper, no one spoke to me. They just stared. I didn't know what was wrong. When I got home, the pastor's wife called me and told me that she wouldn't have done that. I asked her what. She said, "File for a divorce." I said, "Oh! How do you know?" She said, "I saw it in the paper." I dropped the divorce.

A Shakeup in Associated Neighborhood Centers

Oscar started drinking more and more and staying away from work for days without calling to report off. He was the executive director, but he would drink after work with the employees. They would make it to work the next day, but he couldn't. They would laugh about it and tell others about his heavy drinking. Even with his binges, he still kept things going. The final draw was when he stayed off a week without reporting off. Two top people got fired who thought they would benefit from this erroneous behavior of his. His assistant (a friend) reported him, and his secretary joined in with her. The assistant thought she was going to get his job. When he was asked to resign, he fired both of them before he left. He didn't work for two years. It was hard on me and the children. When I got home every day, the house was very clean and dinner cooked and he would have fed the children. I didn't want a house-husband. I wanted a husband who was working because it was time for our son to go to college. I reflected on my home training again, and it was the man who was suppose to take care of the family. Oscar III graduated from high school, and that fall he went away to college in Boston, Massachusetts, to study music. Our son was good and could and can play several instruments.

Our Son Leaves Home Something Bad Got Worse

Oscar III left home and went to school in Boston, seeking a major in percussion instruments. He had a very good first year, and when he came home, he got a job working at General Motors for the summer. Even though he had graduated from high school and in college when he went places, Oscar kept telling him to be home on the weekend at a certain time when he wasn't working. My son woke me up the next morning yelling because he had slept in the car. He told Oscar, "I did come home on time, ask my friends. I couldn't get in and I kept ringing the door bell." I ran out to see what was going on. At the end of the summer, I thought my son was going back to school, but he ran away from home. He and a friend had gone to California. I didn't know where he was, and I thought I would die of grief. I reported him as a missing person. Nothing happened for three months. He called me and told me not to worry about him, that he was all right, and hung up. Three days went by and I didn't hear from him. However, I was thankful that he was all right. He gave me his address and told me to send him some small items to eat because he had been going to the Rescue Mission to eat two meals. I sent him small boxes of cereal and snacks he could eat at other times when he didn't eat at the Rescue Mission. I finally convinced him to come home, but instead he stayed with my sister Wynnifred in Dayton, Ohio, a few weeks before he came home. He was home for a long time before anybody ever spoke about the time when he left home.

Chapter VII
A New Start that Lasted until Retirement

Oscar was working for Children Services after not working for one year and five months. My daughter Wendy said, "Mom, Dad is so mean to you, why don't you leave him?" I told her that the two of us could do more for them than me by myself. She replied, "Mom, you do everything anyway!" I pondered over the idea and realized just how much I was doing. I was so busy helping them and it was getting done, I hadn't noticed. We were working a lot of overtime at General Motors, and I was making more and more money. At work Oscar was doing extremely well. All of his evaluations exceeded expectations. We moved into our dream home in Boardman, Ohio. Wendy went away to school, and it was just the two of us.

By this time Voe was working for the Federal Bureau of Investigation and soon got married. Sharolyn got a full scholarship to law school at the University of Cincinnati. Oscar III was working at The National Institute Of health and soon got married. This gave my husband, it seemed, permission to drink more, come home less, and to help less with the household expenses. He purchased more and more very expensive clothes and things for the house. We would sometimes go shopping together for items for the house. Regardless of what we purchased for the house or what we purchased for ourselves, it was the most expensive item in the store or close to it. He would always make the first two payments and I struggled to pay the rest. He used his money to entertain friends with the most expensive alcohol and buy additional things for himself. It got harder and harder for me to pay all the bills. I found myself working more and more overtime.

Things would really get better for us now, I thought. Wendy was getting married and Sharolyn was graduating from law school within months of each other. I had my speech already memorized as to what I was going to say to Oscar. I was going to tell him that marriage was not a convenience for me; I stayed with him because I loved him and took my marriage vows seriously. The speech didn't happen at all because he came home late and brought company. Time passed, and it was six years later. Now we had three grandchildren and then six years after that we had three more. In all we had a total of six adorable grandchildren—Jay, Javaughn, Docia, Tiffany, Karolyn, and Evan. We enjoyed having the children and grandchildren come home. He could really barbecue, and we really raved about it. In fact, we tried to get him to enter some rib-barbecuing contest, but he never did. We had family gatherings often, and there was no physical abuse, and I had conditioned myself to ignore the verbal abuse.

Monumental Changes
Hard Work Paying Off

I had been taught that any job that is worth your time, it is worth giving it your all. Be your best at whatever you attempt to do. My workload at church increased. I introduced activities and ministries that had never been done at our church. God really used me and prepared me for so many things. I realized my gift even though I had been doing it for a long time was organization and leadership. The pastor would assign me duties, and the end results were beyond your imagination. After my first project, it wasn't hard to get someone to work on my committees because they knew God was going to bless it with success.

I began doing speaking engagements. I called Mom and Dad and asked for assistance. If I needed to know where a scripture was found right away, Dad could tell me and it would give me a chance to talk to them and let them know about the engagement. Mom would have her input, and this is the first speech they helped me with. My life was much different than this speech. I was still living a secret life that I wanted someone to know about other than the children. The first speech was at church for women's day. The title was, "Christian Women Maintaining Their Identity in Today's Society." Some of the things Mom told me to use I couldn't because I was living this secret life. Some things mentioned was being submissive to your husband and allowing him to be the head of the household. She didn't know that I wanted to get away from my husband and not be submissive. I had tried that, and he made things worse for me. It gave him even more control over me. Being submissive when his friends came over was taking me away from what was necessary to do to wait on him and his friends—bring me this or that. His morals and priorities were too different from the ones she and Dad had taught us. Anyway, the speech ended with the congregation standing to their feet applauding.

The Big Layoff

After a few years of being at General Motors, Lordstown, I got laid off for a while, and during this time I read a lot of books on leadership. I also went to a workshop on fundraising and went to a class and learned to do macramé. One day I got a call from the personnel director requesting that I could come in and take the training to be a production supervisor because they were getting ready to hire some more supervisors. I asked him what it entailed. He told me that we would have a written test and do a presentation. I accepted and started making preparations for the presentation. During the time I was looking for information about the company, I decided to do my presentation on, "The Advantages of Having a GM Company in Our Area." Oscar helped me to gather information for the presentation by calling Youngstown State University to see how many of GM employees were having their tuition paid for. He called to find out how many of GM employees had charge accounts and so on. When the day came for me to take the test and do the presentation, he helped me select the right outfit for the occasion. I was happy because he had helped me and this was our project. When the day came for me to go, he hugged me and told me how good I looked and said, "You'll do fine."

Off I went, and everything did go well. It was a very hot day, and on my way I home, I had a flat tire. I stood under the shade until I saw a policeman coming. I flagged him down, and he wanted to know what was wrong. I showed him my flat tire, and he told me that I was close to a service station and I should be able to drive there slowly without damaging my rim. He followed me there and instructed them to help me. It took a while, and finally I was on my way. When I got home I was so excited to tell Oscar about how the presentation went. He wasn't there. I walked through the house and noticed he had moved all of his clothing from the closets. I didn't hear from him for two days. I had all the locks changed so he couldn't just move back in without us having a talk. He sent me half of the house note and a card for each day he was gone. When he came back, he was saying over and over, "I don't know why I acted so stupid. I am all right now."

Called Back To Work

When I was finally got back to work, we both were excited. He started following me. After a week and three days, I couldn't take it anymore. I had to let him know that he was following me. When I pulled in the garage, I looked up and saw him coming from across the street and pulled in the driveway. I asked him why he was following me. He said, "I wanted to make sure you had a flat tire when you told me you did. I haven't found any evidence of it." I showed him the spare tire was still on the rim because I hadn't had any money to buy a new tire. He looked so stupid. As I cooked dinner, he sat there staring into space rubbing his chin as he always would do when he felt bad about something.

Within the first six months after I went back to work, something I had been waiting for a long time finally happened. I got a BA degree from Youngstown State University with an overall grade point average high enough to graduate cum laude. As I look over my transcript, I managed to acquire two 4.0 grade point quarters during my stressful final year. I wanted to do much better, but with the stress and hard work I had been under, this average was worth celebrating! General Motors paid for the final class. Going back to work was rewarding in more ways than one—money for tuition for my son, a degree, a position from which I never got laid off again, and doors that opened to other opportunities. When I graduated, even though I was on the second shift, I managed to make my eight o'clock class every morning. When I was studying, I didn't notice the abuse as much. During this quarter I had to go in one Saturday for a class and when I finished dressing and got ready to leave, Oscar said he was going with me. I said, "Fine!" When we got there, he found out that the instructor was a member of our church. He felt so stupid. He had gone there as a watch dog to make sure I was going to where I said I was going even though I had spent countless hours studying and making preparation for this class.

A Thought for Goal Setters

When you have a goal set and deep within you feel that God has called you to do something bigger and better to accomplish this goal, stay focused! The more you know, the better you will be equipped to handle life challenges. I don't want young women to procrastinate as I did as far as achieving something as valuable as a degree that I was able and knowledgeable to accomplish. My friends tell me, I think to make me feel good, that the time wasn't right. During this time I believe there were missed opportunities that I wasn't recognizing. Whatever a young man says to deter you to do something else, please tell him it can wait. No matter how rosy or sweet he makes it sound, it can wait. If he says, "If you really love me, you can trust me to help you make it happen," say, "No, we can wait." Some of the things that happen to take your attention off your goal might be intentional, especially in cases of abuse. Pray and ask God to lead you in this decision and help you stay on the right path. Ask Him to put people with a worthy purpose in your path or close by when you need someone to talk to. Don't have people who agree with everything you say, such as it is all right, you can do it later. Read your Bible and other good material. You also don't want people who find it necessary to always criticize you. Once you get sidetracked, you may not be as fortunate as I was to continue pressing to get a degree in spite of the circumstances that arose.

Transfer to the Fabrication Plant

The plant next door's office manager went on sick leave. I was asked if I wanted to transfer to the plant next door, the Lordstown fabricating plant. They made some parts for the cars at the assembly plant where I was working and for many other plants and companies. Years had gone by and now it was time to move up from the job as office manager to production supervisor. Sometimes I was asked to be a trainer, which required that you go to Detroit, Michigan, to learn the training and bring it back to teach the other employees. I loved that and hoped it could last all the time. Being a supervisor was nothing like my previous jobs as supervisor. I had to walk like you wouldn't believe. Some of my employees came to really love me and helped me with things that I didn't know about such as working with the union and getting along with the people who kept your line running. That was easy. I wasn't going to show favoritism and smiled, took care of the area's needs, and followed procedures. It almost worked perfectly, but there were three guys who were determined to make waves. I won them over except for one of them, and he was so outnumbered so he almost didn't matter. For some reason they weren't so bad. We got along well most of the time. They referred to me as that little Christian lady or the diva in metal assembly.

By having a BA degree, I was able to apply for the graduate chapter of Alpha Kappa Alpha Sorority, Inc., nominated for the National Association for Female Executives, member of the prestigious Golden Key National Honor Society, and served on the Association Neighborhood Centers Board of Directors. (I returned to help my previous employer.) I continued doing good things at church and at work and moved up from office manager to become a production supervisor. Since I was the junior supervisor, I was put on third shift for maybe a year or more to work in what we called the new building. There were only a handful of people. I would get home on Sunday morning about 7:00 AM, went to bed and got up at 9:30 AM and never missed 11:00 AM service Sunday morning. Oscar stopped going to church during this time. I would tell him when the pastor would ask about him and he acted if it didn't faze him at all.

I didn't like being a supervisor at first. Finally a supervisor was needed on the five door lines. Our best practices and visual aids were always up to date. Our injuries were almost nonexistent. The area consisted of a total of thirty-three people. One of the lines consisted of all women. Even the skilled trade person was a woman named Lenora Solomon. We set the highest production record on one of the lines until the lines changed. I would check occasionally to see if our record stood alone. Dave Chandler, my manager, kept records, and I would have someone check occasionally to see if it had been broken up until 2008. No one has a chance to break it now, for things have changed in the plant tremendously. I am still in contact with some of my former employees who are still working there. We chat and laugh about the good old days—how they rushed to make production and point out the bottlenecks in the system. They were places in the system that always slowed the line down. We still celebrate the time when we set a record and got a free dinner.

A Move to the Safety Department

I had had enough of being a supervisor, and the plant needed some safety engineers to work closely with the employees. The injuries in our plant had become very high. The plant manager thought having safety engineers on each side of the building—one on the pressroom side and the other on the metal assembly side—would get a close up look as to where the most injuries were occurring and get to the root cause and make immediate changes. This was my time to move. I sent my area manager a message, an e-mail, and scheduled a conference. His name was Carl Jones. I went to General Motors Safety Training School in Detroit, Michigan, and became a safety engineer. It was so rewarding and gave me a great deal of exposure that was beneficial in allowing me to do other positive things in safety. Changes begin showing up almost immediately. Within the first year, my partner and I helped to reduce the injuries by 60 percent. Over the next few years, the injuries continued to decrease. Lordstown Metal Center in Lordstown, Ohio, moved from being one of the plants at the bottom in safety up to one of the top plants as far as reduced injuries. I was able to organize and implement many new ideas that made a difference in reducing injuries. The plant manager at the time was Martin Laurent. He was pleased at the results and wrote me a note on the bottom of one of my newsletters that I still save with my certificates stating how pleased he was at the many efforts I was making toward reducing injuries in the offices and on the production floor. He encouraged me to keep up the good work.

During my tenure as a safety engineer, I also traveled extensively to major safety conferences throughout the United States. I even went to Disneyworld in Florida as a representative from General Motors while I attended a conference there. My personnel director could always count on me to bring a written report back. Some of the ideas that I brought back were tried and some were implemented. Some major things happened for me during this time. Out of three shifts and approximately five thousand people I was the first to be nominated at the plant where I worked to participate in Leadership Mahoning Valley. I was shocked and set out to find out who had nominated me.

Afterward it wasn't important anymore; I was so excited about being found favorable for the nomination. I was told by an employee that I would never get in because the only people he knew about who had gotten in were executives or upper management. I told him to count me in because I was going to be selected. He was shocked! Now I was being criticized at home and at work. My congratulatory letter came within two weeks, and this employee was shocked again. I was congratulated by the area managers, the plant manager, and the personnel director, and many others followed when they found out that I had been accepted into Leadership Mahoning Valley. This was considered a very prestigious leadership organization, not just in Mahoning Valley in Ohio but throughout the United States. He was stunned! The personnel director, Jerry Butler, seemed happy because this was the first time anyone from our plant had even been nominated. He made sure my tuition was paid for me to attend the sessions throughout the Mahoning Valley over a nine-month period. After this, I was able to open doors for many other people with God's blessings to go from our plant.

A Recognition That Led to Some Pride

The next recognition that I received was being nominated for the Athena award. I represented our plant, the Lordstown Metal Center. GM is a global industry, and I was the representative from our plant. Imagine me, a girl from the Travis place in Livingston, Alabama. Oscar told me over and over how proud he was of me. He cut my picture out of the paper, laminated it, and enjoyed showing it off. Whenever we went anyplace, he made sure I would wear one of the best-looking outfits and when we would get to the function he would look around the room and whisper in my ear, "You are the best-looking woman here." Afterward he would smile and look happy. When we got home the silence would sometimes start or he would continue talking for days, especially if someone had congratulated me or said something good about me.

By this time in the relationship, Oscar was no longer a quiet drinker; he had to have company over every night. He worked close to home, and every day when I got home there was someone sitting there with him drinking. I would come in and speak and if he wasn't talking to me one friend wouldn't speak either. All the others friends of his would speak and say, "How are you doing, Mrs. Murphy?" I told him that I wanted to have some peace and quiet when I came home and I didn't want to see other people sitting in the house every day. His reply was, "It is my house too."

If things weren't bad enough, I came home from work and not only was someone sitting there, a young man from one of the group homes was out of prison for murder. He had set fire to one of the group homes and caused the death of one of the boys living there. He served his time and when he got out of prison, Oscar allowed him to move in with us. He didn't bother to tell me that he was going to let him move in. I was terrified of him. Everywhere this kid had lived before he had caused trouble. He was adopted twice and it didn't work out. Now he was living in my home. I was afraid to sleep at night. I didn't want to go home. I knew I couldn't stay there. I had to do something. Oscar wasn't going to ask him to leave. He had promised him that he could stay there for a while. So this was my chance to leave. He showed no respect by allowing him to move in and didn't tell me anything about it. The two of them showed up together, and he showed him where he would be sleeping. I had a little talk with God and reminded Him of His promises to me. I told Him that I was really ready to move. I'd had it with this marriage. I didn't want a divorce right now but I wanted to get away, spend some time alone, do some reading, and began writing a book to help other women in my situation. I told God that I had stayed so long because I thought this was my punishment for what I had done—getting married without telling my parents. I asked God for forgiveness, and He told me that He had forgiven me but I never forgave myself. I started making preparations to move. I told Him, "Lord, if I am not doing the right thing, don't let me find an apartment that I will like." The third apartment was the one I fell in love with. Once this happened, again, I gave God a second task because I was told I had to have a credit check. Again, I said, "Lord, if I am not doing the right thing, let this idea fall through at this juncture." Everything went well. I was told to stop by the office and drop off my deposit. I gave God a third task. "Lord, if I am not doing the right thing, don't let me have enough money for the deposit." I had asked one of the tenants that I had seen leaving what the amount of deposit would be and he said a full month's rent plus your current month. I knew this was the breakdown in this move because I didn't have that much money. I went to the rental office anyway, smiling and ready to say, "I don't have that much." I was asked for one hundred dollars. I asked the office manager if she believed in God, and she didn't answer me. I told her that I was going to scream and would it be all right. She said, "Yes." I screamed, *"Thank You, Jesus!"* She told me that once the apartment was cleaned, she would notify me and I would be able to move in at the beginning of the month.

A Day of Reckoning, I Wondered if the Change That I Wanted Would Ever Happen

I told Oscar about how the couples that we used to pal around with had made major changes in their lives—the men had stopped drinking and the couples were taking long vacations together and getting ready for retirement. They were in church. I further said I had put up with the drinking for all these years, put up with the beatings, running to the bank almost daily to cover checks he had written to keep the checks for bills from bouncing, struggling to keep things going and I asked when would my time come for happiness with him, or was it ever coming? He stared that stare and didn't say anything. I suggested that we live on his salary and save mine. He looked at me with hate bursting out of him. I suggested, "Well, let's live off my salary and save yours, and that way if you run short before the next pay, you wouldn't feel hesitant about getting some from the bank." He continued staring at me and said, "No woman can tell me what to do with my money."

I sat there and poured my heart out to God and thought about what I had done to myself and my children. What he had said was right as I sat there thinking, *He is right!* Trying to manage money with him never worked. We could never have a checking account together as I had always seen Mom and Dad have. When we tried to have a checking account together, he would take every penny back out of the account. I had suggested that he pay the bills and handle the money because I didn't mind. I wanted him to see that I was paying all the bills. He didn't want that. He wanted me to continue paying the bills. I thought back, and when he would put his money in the checking account, I called the bank for three years to check the balance to see if he had taken his money out. This would give me time to borrow the money from my friend Naomi Carr to get to the bank before 11:00 AM to pay the shortages because the insufficient checks were returned at 11:00 AM daily. I never got an insufficient payment of $3.00 during those trying times. God was with me as I decided to open a checking account by myself, although it took me approximately three years to stop this check chasing before I got a separate account.

I thought to myself during this time of reckoning that it was time to acknowledge some facts that continued to amaze me all this time. He could always have friends around, but something was always wrong with my friends. They were too this or too that. All those years with him, I did not have a single friend who would come over just to talk to me. If someone wanted to stop over, I would suggest, "Let's meet for lunch," or "I'll see you at sorority meeting or Sunday at church," or "Let's meet at the mall" in order to avert the visit. My one friend Elizabeth Jenkins came anyway when we were working on a project, and most time he would walk in and wouldn't speak to her. If a woman came, she was always with her husband. Not one woman came alone for years unless she came to see both of us! It was time to make that move that would surprise a multitude of people that I had fooled for much too long. And now he had allowed this guy that I was terrified of to move into my house. Our dream house didn't mean anything anymore. I was leaving.

Although I was still thinking about what people would say, it didn't bother me anymore. The move was ready to become a reality without any fuss. I thought about the time I came home from work and as I pulled in the driveway, I saw my clothes had been thrown out of the second-floor window. It came to me about the time I was locked out of the bedroom for a month and was locked out the house at one time and had to call the police to get in. When they got there, the only thing that was said when he let me in was, "Do you love him?" and they left before I gave them an answer. I repeated again, it is time for that permanent move.

I recalled many things that should have been nipped in the bud, as my Dad would say, but it was too late. The night my youngest daughter was embarrassed the night of her prom because he was passed out in the foyer drunk and we tried to get him up stairs before her friends came to pick her up. This wasn't easy, but it had to be done! I thought of leaving the dream house, and that is what it had come to be—the dream house, not our dream house. It was a flop house for him and his friends to lie around in and party.

PART VI

THE UNVEILING OF MY SECRET LIFE

Chapter VIII
The Move that Changed My Life Forever and I Unveiled My Secret Life

Almost forty years had passed. I talked to God as I had so often done in the past. "Lord, Moses was in the wilderness for forty years. It rained on Noah and the ark forty days and forty nights; my forty years of this craziness is approaching, and there are more years of life behind me than before me, so I want You to be the leader in this undertaking. This time, Lord, the move is going to happen." The children were gone, and I had made a promise that I was going to leave when the children got grown. Not only were they grown, but they all were married and living out on their own and with children of their own. I would turn sixty years old in August, and it was time to make this move that I had so often thought about. I was going to keep Oscar on my insurance because mine was better than his. I had come to the realization a long time ago that he wasn't going to change, and even though he would stop drinking for long periods, I realized that he really didn't want to stop drinking. He never changed friends who were really not good for him. He couldn't see that. Who would come and sit at someone's house day after day knowing you had a wife who didn't drink and didn't want you there? All respect for me was gone, even from his friends. Even if it was all right with him to be at my house day after day, what about empathy for others?

I started making plans to move. The children were told, and they were very supportive. I had put aside some money and had found an apartment. I also had put some furniture in lay-away. I prayed and asked God again that if I was doing the right thing to let things go smooth for me, and they did. I left him the dream house and ninety-five percent of the things in it. I moved two months before our fortieth wedding anniversary. He told people that I'd be back. I took all the bills with me that I knew about and helped him to pay the house note for two months. I continued to pay the charge cards until they were paid in full.

He only had utilities, his food, and the house note. After the very first month I had so much money left over, I was surprised. I went over and over the bills to make sure I didn't miss anything. While living there, I rarely had any money and was never allowed to change anything at our dream house. He would tell me, "You have learned to dress nicely, but you don't know crap about decorating a house." He loved that house, and I left and made a fresh start. I had finally made a permanent move after all those years. I know the angels in heaven were applauding.

Life after Abuse

I moved to an apartment that was about a mile or a little less away so it wouldn't be hard for the children and grandchildren to come visit us. The furniture was delivered, and I put up draperies to keep people from being able to look in because I lived on the first floor. I was lonely living alone for several months, but it was worth it. There was peace and quietness. I could go home and no one was sitting there drinking and playing loud music. However, I was determined not to ever go back. That is one thing I never did was to pack my clothes and leave and then come back. He didn't take me seriously when I told him when the children got grown I was going to stop putting up with his mess. Had I told him that I was going to move he probably would have said, "Yeah, right" and even laughed in m face. I knew he would never move no matter how much I begged him to do so because he loved that house and he wouldn't have taken me seriously because of the hurt he had put me through and I stayed.

What Will Mom and Dad Say?

By now I was wondering how my dad the preacher and the supportive mom would take this move I had made. Neither was told until I was in the apartment for a while. When friends called for a long time, I found out that Oscar was telling them that I wasn't available or would tell them that he would tell me to call them or I wasn't there. He was embarrassed to tell them that I had left. I called my mom and told her I had moved and asked her not to tell dad yet. She said, "I don't like to keep things about our children from him." After I told her, I ended by saying, "Mom, when you adjust to it, then you tell Dad." She said all right. I heard about leaving every time I talked to her, and we talked every Sunday morning before getting ready for church. I had told her many times before that I was going to leave but only told her that he drank too much. She would say, "You better stay with your husband." This time, I still didn't tell her anything other than I had moved. "You shouldn't have left your husband," she replied. "He was always nice and respectful to us." I said, "Yes, but you don't live with him." After a year, Mom told Dad. He wanted to know what happened after forty years. I told him the whole story about the abuse and drinking. He was so happy I had moved out. "What took you so long? Didn't I tell you not to stay with anybody who would hit you or be mean to you? Your mom and I had done a good job raising you!" He asked me over and over, "What did you say happened?" My father was happy I had finally made this move. He told me that it was my fault because the abuse and drinking should have been nipped in the bud from the beginning. My mom said, "You didn't tell me all that!" I saw why she had me put the things in my speech that I had asked her to help me write in years earlier. Dad shared with me that years earlier, when I was a very small kid, he'd had to dismiss one of his deacons for abusing his wife. He went on to share the whole story with me.

Whenever Dad visited other churches, he always acknowledged Mom and followed that with something very special. He would say she was the cream in his coffee, the butter on his bread, etc. She always said that she was so embarrassed by these acknowledgments.

After moving, for some time on the way home I picked myself up something from one of the fast food chains, ate, got ready for bed, read the newspaper, some pages in a book I had started, watched the news, and went to bed. I stopped opening the draperies and didn't talk to anybody in my building for fear of being questioned about who I was and where I came from. I didn't want them to know that I had moved from that nice house about a half mile away. However, I was able to get a good night's sleep. This is something that I hadn't been able to do for a long time. Just before I moved, the drinking had increased and visits every evening after work. I could tell when the alcohol was taking over because voices and music got louder. Sometimes when company left he'd fall asleep wherever they were sitting. Sometimes I could wake him up to go to bed and there were times when I couldn't. I would walk in quietly and turn the music off. He would wake right up and say, "I am listening to that." He would go and turn it back on at times. I would go to bed about 9:00 PM, and with all the getting up to turn off the record player my mornings sometimes felt almost as if I had just gone to bed. I was tired all the time, and I had headaches badly. Prescription medicine did not stop my headaches but would only quiet them down so I could function.

Now that I was sleeping well at night without any interruptions, I noticed my headaches were gone. I needed to go the doctor to get my medicine for headaches because I was all out. I continued to realize I didn't have a headache. In fact, I hadn't had one for several weeks after I had moved. I made a doctor's appointment anyway and I told him what had happened and that I had left Oscar. He looked sad. He had been our family doctor for over thirty years. Dr. Hernandez knew the children and remembered their names and would ask about them. He told me that Oscar was in to see him recently and he had one of the worst bladder infections he had ever seen. He went on to say that if he didn't stop drinking it was going to kill him. The doctor checked me out and what was thought to be a major sinus problem turned out to be something different. It was that I was allergic to smoke and some was stress. I also had indigestion even from drinking water sometimes. As

I write this book, which is over a period of eleven years in the making, I have had very few headaches and very little indigestion. I believe my health is close to where it should be for my age except for high blood pressure and arthritis that I manage with exercise, proper foods, and rarely a pain pill. *There is life after abuse!*

Retirement for Oscar

Oscar retired from Mahoning County Children Services after twenty-four years. There was a party for him. I knew being home his drinking would get worse and I was glad that I had moved and wouldn't be there to witness such outpouring of his friends. He was retired and had more time to do nothing but drink and play loud music. If he fell asleep without eating, he could do that for days. For a while employees would still come to the house for help. I suggested to him to charge consultant fees. He said that they were going to set up something like that. I don't know if they ever did. His former employees/friends still came to sit and drink even though he was in bad health and wasn't supposed to be drinking or smoking. He had had a stroke and had other things wrong. I found out that he hadn't driven for several years. It sounds as if I am blaming them for his continued drinking, but I am not. He was grown and very intelligent. He was a very good social worker. He could read a book and summarize it for you without referring back other than for footnotes. Some people would have had to go back and reread something to write a good report but not him. He got it the first time. His writing skills were almost perfect.

Visits from the Children

When the children came home, I told them that they could bring their dad down to my apartment with them if he wanted to come. He loved the children and grandchildren and enjoyed spending time with them when his friends weren't around. After the first time he came down, when he got back home he called me and told me he was surprised when he walked in the apartment and saw how pretty it was. "I didn't know it was in you. I sat there in awe." I told him that he criticized everything I did and never gave me a chance. He was silent and said goodbye. He purchased two very expensive vases as housewarming gifts, and I stopped by to pick them up. They matched the décor perfectly.

When he had a stroke, the children asked me if I would stay at the house until he got well enough to take care of himself. I told them no, but I would take him to my apartment. I took him there and took care of him until it was safe for him to be alone at home. Again he was surprised because I was being so nice to him. He had nothing but praise for me. When it was time for him to leave, he didn't try to stay. He hugged me, said thanks over and over, and left. On Sunday I picked him up for church for about two years. Sometimes we would have dinner after church as friends sometimes do. He eventually stopped going to church again.

Retirement and Move for Me

About three years before I would retire, I came to Upper Marlboro, Maryland, purchased a lot, and built a new home. I took the same approach as I did when I was getting ready to move in the apartment from the dream house. Had not I taken the same approach, I would have had to ask Oscar to sell the house, and I didn't want to do that. I wanted him to always have a place to stay, and he definitely did not want to move. The developer had five models to choose from, and I wanted one of the two largest. I said to God that I didn't want approval for the house I really liked if I couldn't afford it and be able to keep it. That was something that Bells (my maiden name) just didn't do—get more than they could afford. He confirmed my request over and over and over that I could afford it until the day I was called to go to closing. It took almost the whole three years for the house to be ready, which was fine, because I was still working. I wanted to move to Maryland in order to be near family because I didn't have any relatives in Ohio. Oscar and I were separated and living very different lives. My brother Clarence suggested to Oscar that since I was moving to Maryland that he should sell the house and also get closer to family. His response was, "All my friends are here, and she is not going any place. I am going to stay here." I moved to Upper Marlboro in September 2003, and he died two months later, November 19, 2003. He was skin and bones and didn't look like the person I had seen two months earlier.

Oscar's Death

Oscar's death was a shock to everyone. He didn't die from alcohol; he died from an aneurysm. Two of the children were able to get to the hospital before he died, but he had slipped into a coma. I arrived shortly after dinner, and he never knew we were there. He died the next day. When he was picked up by the undertaker we went back to the house. I went to the bedroom where we slept and just stood there and looked around the room. I reminded God that I had prayed for him to stop drinking and it never happened. Although people told me that they would see him at different churches, he never became active again in Antioch Baptist Church. I asked God why. Even though he had stopped drinking many times, why not when he had so many things wrong with him? Why, Lord, was he never healed, because the doctor told me that his blood level was 30 percent alcohol? A voice spoke to me clearly. God is too wise to make a mistake and too just to do wrong. I dropped my head and left the room. With that being said, it helped me to get through the funeral preparations. He was sixty-eight years old. I notified all his relatives and my siblings. I then told my parents about his death, and they were very sad and sent flowers and a card to be read. It was during the Thanksgiving holidays, and my siblings were in Livingston, Alabama, to spend Thanksgiving with Mom and Dad, a practice we had done for many years. However, my brother Clarence, who is a judge now, and my sister Wynnifred, who had retired from General Motors, came to represent the family. Six years later, he is still talked about at family gatherings.

The Funeral

At his funeral, there was an outpouring of friends from near and far who came to pay their last respects. The service was a wonderful home-going celebration. His former supervisor collected personal items to name a conference room at Mahoning County Children Services for Oscar. He was good at what he did at work. He was loved and respected. Years before he retired, he was supervisor of the Residential Homes for Boys. The children loved him dearly. Sometimes he would bring children home, and they all would ask us to adopt them. We didn't adopt them, but they knew they could always come to visit. After the funeral, his body was brought back to Upper Marlboro, Maryland, and is buried here in the Resurrection Cemetery. His legacy lives on. The good things are well documented not just where he worked but in the hearts and minds of so many people.

A Decline in My Parent's Health

Dad was a preacher for sixty-nine years and a pastor for fifty-eight years, with a stroke causing him to retire. It didn't stop him from preaching because we got a sermon often, and so did anyone else who came to visit him. As Dad's illness progressed over a few years, we managed to keep him at home until three months before he died. He had so much wisdom and natural intelligence. He had a vast vocabulary that made us proud. All our trips home became more frequent. I got to spend forty-one days with him before he died. By this time Mom was in a wheelchair, but I managed to get her to the hospital or rehabilitation center three or four times a week. When I rolled her in his room, his face would light up and he would reach for her hands. She would sit there and they would rub each other's hands. He wanted her to stay as she had done in the past, but she told him that she had gotten too old and wasn't able to do that now.

On one of the days when I didn't take Mom with me and he was getting weak, he looked at me with my arms folded looking out the window, and he said, "Don't grieve for me. I have had a good life. I married a good wife. God blessed me with eight good children, and all of you have made me proud. You have done great things for me, and I thank you. I don't want you to ever forget about Mama. I don't have a lot of money to leave you all, but I am leaving you my *good name!*" This dispels some of the myths about preachers' kids being some of the worst kids. I will say about 90 percent are not bad children. You see, a handful is bad, and then others brand all of us with the same adjectives. How unfortunate!

As I sit here weeping, I also know there are good marriages. I saw one, and I know there are many others. When Dad said he was leaving us his good name, he did. Had he done anything immoral, we would have heard about it. Livingston is a small town, and everybody seems to know what is happening in everybody's life. He and my mom loved each other unconditionally and were married seventy years and three months. There were no closet-children showing up and demanding to be seated with the family at the funeral. He loved Mom until he took his last breath, Tuesday, March 13, 2007, three months and a few days short of his ninety-second birthday. When I am home now, my mom and I share funny stories about Dad. He would tell jokes and would laugh so hard that when he had finished, we didn't know what he was talking about. Mom is ninety-two years old and is in fair health and misses Dad immensely!

Multiple Deaths Close Together

Beginning in January 2003 through March 2007, I struggled with several deaths of people who were very close to me. I know God is not a respecter of persons and He is too wise to make a mistake and too just to do wrong. I mourned for the loss of eight people over a period of four years. Just when I felt relief, not over, just relief from one there was the death of another and another. I will not use this space for a pity party because God has been my Bridge Over Troubled Waters, Burden Bearer, Heavy Load Carrier, and Comforter in the time of heartbreak when it felt like something was pulling my heart out of my chest and my flesh crawling. During times of loneliness, He said, "I am with you now and forever." I said goodbye to my first cousin mentioned earlier, Richard Hall, my forty-two-year-old son-in-law James Talley Jr., and my husband, Oscar Murphy Jr. in 2003 at age sixty-eight. Over the next three years, it was my brother, Dwight L. Bell Jr., who was only a year and nine months younger than me, my church mom, Mrs. Sadie Bibbs, and her son, Willie Bibbs, five months apart, and three weeks later, my dad, Reverend Dwight L. Bell Jr, and a friend from church that I called Ms Myrtle but her last name was White. During this time I have been able to reach out to so many people in my situation. With help, I have had four educational conferences since moving to Maryland that have been a big help to me as well as others. They were also spiritually, socially, and economically helpful through well-informed speakers. I have received many calls saying, "Thank you, that was just what I needed."

Absorbed in Thought Again, Recall – Noticing Abuse Early

For some reason, when someone was abused, it stood out in my thoughts beginning in high school. I didn't know why then but I do now. God was letting me know that He had something special for me to do. Now was the time for me to do something other than just move out and free myself from the abuser. I had to do something for other women. I started visualizing things that had stood out in my mind for many years. We were in the ninth grade and this couple spent so much time together. They were the talk of the class. One day at lunch he was waiting for her and when she got there he slapped her and gave her a nickel and told her to go get her some gum because her breath was stinking. She took it and went and got the gum.

Another classmate would tell me, occasionally, that her boyfriend would beat her when they were out over the weekend. Sometimes she would say, "Carolyn, he beat me so badly this weekend," and she would laugh about it. I didn't get that.

When children came to school I could tell if they came from an abusive home. They would sometimes fall asleep in school. If I asked them if they went to bed late, they would say, "No, don't tell them I told you, but Daddy was fighting Mommy last night and I was scared and couldn't sleep." I showed them as much love as I could short of reporting it.

Later in life, one time I did report abuse in a family and this child's mother was a well-known teacher and nothing happened. I was told to mind my own business.

By now, I was obsessed with learning about abuse, and when it was brought to my attention or if I experienced it, I knew there was a way to make things better. After twenty-three years of serious research, I became knowledgeable about abuse, could recite data readily, and was getting old. I knew I had to do something and didn't know exactly what. I had gone to workshops, retreats, Al-Anon, and conferences. During the conferences and retreats, battered women would come together and wonder why there were no topics on abuse. We shared our horror stories and other information with each other during breaks. God had a way of bringing us together as He prepared me for something very special. I continued with my determination to learn more and more about a variety of different areas of expertise. Not only did I want to be able to talk about abuse and areas surrounding work and church, but I also wanted to be able to join in a variety of areas such as health, current events, and other major topics during the particular time in history. My family concluded that I was going to be a professional student, meaning that as long as I lived I was going to seek some way to organize or attend classes on some major subject. I have come to that conclusion also. It has been made clear to my children that when I am a hundred years old, and if I am unable to walk, I want them to dress me up and put on my heels, a great suit, an outstanding hat, great-smelling cologne, and red lipstick and push me to a conference or class. If possible, I want to be able to be one of the presenters. I hope you are laughing now as hard as I am!

Women's Conference

There was a women's conference at Sharolyn's church in Philadelphia, Pennsylvania, about two years earlier, and she invited me to come up. Since it was a six-hour drive, I had asked Oscar if he would ride up with me for company, and he said no. I drove six hours to and from the conference alone and went to the three-day conference at Freedom Christian Bible Fellowship Church. The presenters were outstanding. The keynote speaker who was on program spoke on domestic abuse. A pastor's wife finally came to Philadelphia and addressed domestic violence in the worst way. This lady was actually a pastor's wife. She didn't read a book; she experienced it and had signs to prove it. When she finished, there wasn't a dry eye in the audience. Most of the audience was weeping—some were bawling out loud. She wrote a book entitled, *I Suffered in Silence.* This is when I began to hear more and more horror stories about abuse. Without a doubt, I knew I had to do something! Hearing what this woman said and my personal experience—oh yes, the time was right. I was not going to let another chance pass without reaching out to those of us who were suffering in silence.

On my way home, I felt as if someone was sitting beside me. I know it was God's presence. You will have to be a Christian to understand what I am going to say. My inner thoughts said, "You don't have to drive this far for this kind of conference. You can do this at home." When I reached my driveway, I had the whole organization planned. I knew who I was going to ask to help me, where we would meet, our colors and what they stood for, and our theme. I also had my mission statement memorized and a place in mind to have the first meeting. I pulled in my garage and ran in and started writing everything down. I remembered the verse in Habakkuk 2:2 (KJV) that states, "And the Lord answered me, and said, Write the vision, and make it plain upon tables, that he may run that readeth it." I had everything done except the name for the organization. This trip will always be visualized in my mind. They were special moments with God, and I had a lot of them. I started getting up at 4:30 every morning so I could have a half hour of uninterrupted time with God before getting ready for work. This time would consist of prayer, reading from my Bible, and *The Thought for Today*. After retiring, I still do.

PART VII

MAKING A DIFFERENCE

Chapter IX
The Beginning of Women of Excellence NWAS, Inc.

I made a list of the women who I would contact. I called them and followed up with a letter about the first meeting. In April 1998, we came together for our first meeting at the Youngstown Club at 202 Commerce Street in Youngstown, Ohio. My vision was shared with Marty Bushy, Esq., Leonora Solomon, Barbara Pennington, Jessie Peterson, Janice Baldwin, Marie Danes, Lynnette Sutton, and Mildred McElroy. Marie Danes and Barbara Pennington came up with the name Women of Excellence NWAS, Inc. The organization was in operation three months after inception. We had received our incorporation approval. The first project was a weekend retreat at the Holiday Inn on Belmont Avenue in Youngstown, Ohio. Guests came from near and far to attend the beginning of a group designed to meet the needs of all women. Both major newspapers in Youngstown carried articles about the organization and plans for the retreat. The *Buckeye Review* carried an article and a picture of the group, and the *Youngstown Vindicator* carried a large article. The weekend retreat was a success. In fact, years later it is still being talked about when we come together or see an attendee we haven't seen in a long time.

Women of Excellence NWAS, Inc. is a 501c3 non-profit organization who reaches out to women from all walks of life beginning with middle school girls. Within the differences you will find different cultures, different denominations, and different educational backgrounds that have come together as one to enhance the total woman. Our goal is to enhance the total woman spiritually, educationally, economically, and socially. This enhancement is done through workshops, retreats, mentoring, referrals, and scholarships addressing spiritual issues, feminist ethics, and political and social issues. Another major function of the organization is to educate women beginning with middle school girls about the different kinds of abuse before a relationship enters the danger zone. I want them to know danger signs to watch for and to encourage independence and know when it is necessary before it is too late. It is not the organization's desire to separate couples but empower women to make the best decisions for them. It is also not a desire to replace any organization but to offer an alternative with a different approach.

We are not a social organization by any means or just another abuse organization. Women who contact us or show up at our functions will never show up at a shelter or a regular support group or even bother to call the domestic hotline. They come to trust us because we do not share their information. However, if they come to the point where they want to share the information, they do so with power and might, and this has happened over the past ten years.

Since its inception, the organization has focused a lot on abuse, verbal and physical. We are trying to raise the awareness for the need for women to feel good about themselves and exercise independence when the need is there—don't compromise! For the past eleven years we have touched the lives of thousands of women. Many of them have told me to start the awareness as early as middle school because when a lot of women get in their forties or older, they feel as though they have invested too much time in the relationship to walk away. It is harder when children are involved. Even when things are very intense, I have been told that they were going to try to stick it out because there are more years behind them than before them. I weep for these women. I know everyone deserves happiness. What they don't know or realize that happiness begins within oneself. It comes from within, and you are in this partnership with God to make it happen!

After five years and being asked by supporters if they made a contribution, whether or not it would be tax deductible, we decided to become a 501c3 organization. During this time paying someone to fill out a 501c3 application was very costly. It was a means for Women of Excellence NWAS, Inc., to compete for local, state, and federal funds. Several companies or individuals were contacted for a price quote. The price quoted was more than we could afford. I decided to fill out the application myself. The naysayers emerged again. They shared with me that if I submitted an application and it wasn't approved, my application would go to the bottom of the list and it would take some time for it to come up for review again. It didn't stop me from filling out the application myself. It took me about two weeks to do the application myself, but I was determined to do it because the organization couldn't afford the prices that were being asked to complete the application.

The application was submitted and it took a while to get a response. I called the Internal Revenue Service to keep track of the process. Everyone I talked to was very friendly and told me how far it was along and let me know that there were many others who submitted applications and they were answered in the order they were received. I finally got the message and stopped calling. Then one day the letter came with the answer. It laid on the kitchen counter a couple of days and as I was passing by, I took the letter in my hands and held it to my chest and took a deep breath. It stated what I had been hoping for—the organization met the guidelines for being a 501c3 organization. We were so excited. The first question was, "Who did the application for you?"

I was too happy to say I did it myself. Well, not quite—with my Heavenly Father as the overseer!

Some of the Rewards from the Organization

Working for women is so rewarding. It keeps me very busy, and I am so happy when I have helped a group of woman by raising awareness about abuse, verbal and physical. It feels as if my whole body is happy and each organ is rejoicing on its own. Look at some of the things the organization is doing. (1) Temporary housing—calls have come in from temporary shelters that are filled and we have been asked to put victims up in a hotel for a night or longer to give the abuser a chance to cool off. (2) Scholarships—when there has been a need to help with tuition and pay for attendance at a conference where abuse is being discussed. (3) Counseling or just being there. Some women need someone to listen and pray with them, nothing else. (4) Employment—we have talked to supervisors about change of job to aid the victim so she can be independent. (5) Supply pertinent items—we have donated clothing and toiletries. (6) Referrals—if we can't help we know where to refer them. (7) Mentoring—there is nothing like having a good role model to take the journey with you. It prevents young women from being clueless about abuse, especially if you have lived a sheltered life or where it is prevalent.

In 2007 as I was looking at the *Early Show*, I noticed that the Domestic Hotline was celebrating its twelfth anniversary. It was stated that over 1.3 million women had called the hotline. That is an astonishing number, but there are about that many who did not call during that same time period. In the life of Women of Excellence NWAS, Inc., there have been only a handful of women who stated that they had called the hotline. It is a big secret in families. What happens there usually stays there until sometimes it is too late. I know this is my calling. I have had silent periods, but as one writer stated, "When God wants you to do something, it won't go away. It is like trick candles on a birthday cake, you keep blowing them but they won't go away" (author unknown).

My love for doing things to meet the needs of women has spilled over into doing things for other causes for women. I don't turn down any invitations to speak or share my story with other women. I also sympathize with men when they tell me that they have been abused. During the presidential campaign, I worked to help elect President Barack Obama and Vice President Joe Biden because I thought and felt deeply that they were better candidates for us and they had openly spoken out for things to help women. This was a first for me, working for a presidential campaign. It was a win-win opportunity because I was able to network with so many others and hear their stories and share mine. I support all functions to raise money to fund cures for different diseases and the list goes on.

Intimate Moments with God

I Am Thankful

I am thankful, dear God, for Your love and for how You have shown it throughout my entire lifetime.

I thank You for keeping me through all those years when I was taking care of the family and not taking care of myself.

I thank You for watching over me when I tried over and over to fix things my way instead of letting You lead the way and I follow.

I thank You for Your grace and mercy, the know-how, and allowing me through Your grace and mercy another chance to get right whenever I messed up.

I thank You for keeping my soul and my mind together, which kept me from getting hooked on the things of the world early in my marriage that others sometimes do, such as bars, alcohol, and other horrible things to please others.

I thank You for favor and bringing me safely to this moment in life while experiencing miracles reserved just for me.

I thank You for the successes, no matter how large or small.

I thank You for the values we have instilled in our children and for causing them to pass them down to their children.

I thank You for Mom and Dad who taught us that if you keep God's commandments, He will not only bless you but He will bless your children and your children's children!

I thank You for my entire family.

I thank You for the love I have for my family.

I am thankful that it is not a casual love but a deep down love that brings me to my knees daily to pray for them.

I also thank You for how You kept me when I didn't take advantage or recognize the missed opportunities to get away from my abuser.

I thank You for the wisdom and knowledge that I have acquired from the toils and snares of my life.

I am thankful, dear Lord! I am thankful!

Amen!

My Favorite Scriptures for Intimate Moments with God

All scriptures are from the King James Version of the Bible.

Psalm 37

"Fret not thyself because of evildoers, neither be thou envious against the workers of

iniquity ..." I don't fret because of those who try to intimidate me or destroy my faith in God.

Psalm 34: 1

"I will bless the Lord at all times: his praise shall continually be in my mouth." Through all the good times and all the bad times, I have learned to praise the Lord. It heightened each situation. When things were good my praises made them better. When they were bad, I praised Him because I could feel that He was right there with me and it was just a matter of time before the circumstances were sure to change.

Psalm 23

"The Lord is my shepherd, I shall not want ..." He is my everything.

Psalm 147:3

*"He heals the broken-hearted, and binds up their wounds."*_Thank you, Lord, for keeping your promise.

Psalm 121

"I will lift up mine eyes unto the hills, from whence cometh my help ..." When all else fails, I know what to do.

I also love stories about distinguished women in the Bible, and there are many. I have some favorites that I have never heard mentioned other than in Bible study --The daughters of Zelophehad. They are Mahlah, Noah, Hoglah, Milcah, and Tirzah, and they are talked about in Numbers 27 ... They give me determination.

Sarah, Abraham's wife, is one of my favorites, a woman of faith, courage, and vision. There are other women who are not named, but mentioned as *"the woman" and ...*

I also love to hear success stories about women in all walks of life. My heart screams with prayers for them.

My Special Project An Ongoing Visual Aid in Schools— an Organization/Club

There is need for an organization or class beginning in every middle school through high school addressing physical and verbal abuse. It is not enough to have someone show up once or twice a year to give a lecture on abuse. There needs to be an ongoing visual aid as an organization and class similar to the Science Club, Future Teachers, and Junior Achievement, although I'd rather that abuse become a class as other classes. They need to know about these horrible actions that can put a damper on life or totally destroy it. The students should be allowed to wear the colors symbolizing abuse as they do colors for other things to be an ongoing reminder that abuse is a no-no.

Suggestions for Implementation of an Organization/Club

Below are suggestions for implementing an organization, some warning signs of verbal and physical abuse, a history of abuse from the preacher's kid, and a lesson plan to aid in your implementation.

The organization doesn't have to be called Women Of Excellence NWAS, Inc., but it would be nice. The NWAS in our name stands for not without a struggle. Use a name that the students will be comfortable with, but use the same concept, colors, and motto. Organize your organization according to *Robert's Rules of Order*. We have by-laws, but you can adjust yours to fit your school or send for ours as a reference.

Use our intake process—Women of Excellence NWAS, Inc.

Something is needed to assure or encourage dedication.

The colors are purple and white:

Purple stands for royalty because we are children of the Almighty God and shaped in His image.

White stands for purity. We are always striving for excellence and to become pure and holy.

Our mottos are:

"Women Helping Women." Help other women to keep from making the same mistakes others have made. Sometimes they just want you to listen. Don't be pushy; you will lose them when they are needed.

" More than conquerors ..." (Romans 8:37). Always aspire to be an overcomer. There is nothing too hard for God.

Educational Information, Lesson Plan and Tools to Work With for Globalization Against Abuse Toward Women

Some of the Warning Signs for Physical and Verbal Abuse

As I look back over my life, I see all the warning signs listed on the Internet stated by Dr. Irene Matiatos with one of her clients. I have to get the word into our schools. I want to start as early as middle school. I don't want young girls totally clueless about physical and verbal abuse. It tears one down, and you don't bounce back as quickly as you want to. It has to be stopped before the wounds are too deep. My strong relationship with God kept me above water. I get so many compliments about my strength, my beauty, my sense of humor, my boldness and smartness, and I have learned to say thank you! I don't get the feeling that I am being set up for the nest to fall! I get asked to speak for different functions but not about abuse because of the secret I so tightly kept a lid on. Only the children and I knew and one of my pastors that I had for thirty-eight years. He loved us dearly and wanted so badly for things to work out. He never suggested divorce. He counseled us off and on for years and tried to break the silence once by inviting us over for dinner one afternoon. I told him that Oscar hadn't talked to me in weeks and I wasn't going to sit at the table and break bread with him. He would talk to me as if everything was all right and when we got back home the silence returned as soon as we got in the house.

From Dr. Irene Matiatos List of Warning Signs of Verbal and Emotional Abuse (The Ones I Experienced).

See the entire list at www.obygn.net

These warning signs are throughout my story:

- gives you the silent treatment
- ignores your feelings
- disrespects you
- withholds approval, appreciation, or affection
- walks away without answering you
- criticizes you, calls you names, yells at you
- humiliates you privately or in public
- rolls his eyes when you talk
- gives you hard times about socializing with your friends or family
- presents a wonderful face to the world and is well liked by outsiders
- twists your words, somehow turning them against you
- tries to control decisions, money, even the way you style your hair or wear your clothes
- complains about how badly you treat him
- threatens to throw you out
- ever pushes or hits you, even "accidentally"
- promises never to do something hurtful again
- harasses you about imagined affairs
- questions your every move and motive, somehow questioning your competence
- makes you feel like you can't win; like you're damned if you do, damned if you don't
- incites you to rage, which is "proof" that you are to blame

My situation became so critical that I found myself walking on eggshells. When I talked I talked slowly to make sure I got the words

I thought he would want to hear to avoid any backlash. I never got it right. If he gave me the silent treatment, I wondered how long it would go on and when he would be loving and talkative again. As I finish the signs that I recognized from Dr. Matiatos, I wish I had a dollar for the times when I made excuses for him.

A Very Common Sign that Stands Out

When I am networking, one very common sign of abuse is when I introduce myself, share one of my cards, and give a brief summary about what the organization is about, sometimes a victim will share a story supposedly about a friend or relative. As I listen carefully, the person will slip and use first person to describe a particular incident with details that only a victim would know.

Aid for a Special Group—Military Wives

While volunteering for the presidential campaign, I interfaced with several military workers who told me how prevalent abuse is among the wives of servicemen and asked me to see if there is something I could do for them. My immediate response was that we can help anybody as long as they want to be helped and will let us. I am being creative and trying to complete my research to find more ways to meet the needs of abused women. And I am being successful.

Under the Next Section You Will See a Lesson Plan to Make It Easier to Teach a Class and Organize a Group

Physical and Verbal Abuse
History of Abuse by the Woman of Excellence/Preacher's Kid
Carolyn Bell Murphy

Physical and verbal abuse, *I think,* originated as a misinterpretation of the Holy Bible: "For the ***husband*** *is the head of the* ***wife,*** even as Christ is the head of the church: and He is the Savior of the body" (Ephesians 5:23, KJV). This is one of the scriptures I have heard being quoted and used to justify this behavior and sometimes used as a major cause leading to abuse and reason to control women. This verse is grossly over stated and misinterpreted. The entire verse is not analyzed in its entirety to bring out the clarity demonstrated. Readers stop the interpretation too soon with one phrase—*husband is the head of the wife. This scripture is probably used mostly by Christians to justify abuse. It is an act that is used by some pastors or other heads of church and many other people.*

I did hours of research trying to find out what culture and an approximate date as to when domestic abuse began. Not being able to find the exactness of this horrible act is not very important, but *ending* it is major! I believe that when one culture started abusing their women, it started a ripple effect and somehow other groups adopted it.

Abuse comes in two forms, verbal and physical, and is an ancient tradition that is sometimes passed down generation after generation. It is a learned behavior. It is a form of control and is defined by Webster's Dictionary[1] as "misuse, to hurt by treating wrongly; to speak as in coarse or bad terms of or to; immoral or dishonest practice or act."

1 Landau, Sidney, edit. *Webster's Dictionary.* Chicago: J G Ferguson Publishing Company, 1978.

Men have stated that verbal and physical abuses are means to keep women straight week after week. The word *husband* in Ephesians 5:23 is substituted for *male* and the word *wife* is substituted for *female.* This gives men (they say) the authority over women.

It would be interesting to share some information with the class to show why this class is important. The woman of excellence had no idea that abuse existed between married couples until it happened to her.

Lesson Plan for Abuse Beginning in Middle School

Why middle school? Middle school is the age when girls begin making decisions about dating. After an ongoing survey, when asked by teens if they had witnessed physical abuse, verbal abuse, both, or experienced any or all, responses were almost spontaneous. Overwhelmingly, the responses were yes! The responses came before the question was completed 90 percent of the time.

Objective:

1. To raise the awareness of abuse at an early age.
2. To introduce and recognize the warning signs.
3. To do something about the signs from the beginning.
4. To elevate self-esteem and dangers of abuse being an acceptable behavior.
5. To introduce the value of oneself.
6. To be emphatic and stick to *no* when confronted.
7. To report this behavior to the proper authorities *right away* (police, doctors, social worker, school counselors, pastors/heads of church, and friends). Some of my research has revealed that sometimes pastors/heads of church or policemen are not the safest people to report to because they have been found to be abusers themselves. I hope this is a very small group of people. (I think it is overstated about pastors.)
8. To help students feel at ease talking about abuse with parents. Research has shown where abuse is practiced in the home, the children are least likely to mention it until they are teens and ask mom, "Why are you taking that abuse?" and sometimes the boys will begin fighting the father and some will go as far as to kill him.

Introduction:

Beginning with the first class, physical and verbal abuse should be defined with examples. Give an overview of what to expect from the class and how quizzes will be handled.

Share information about the woman of excellence, not without a struggle, who feels that this is a must-have class if we are going to minimize domestic abuse. Share something about her good life and the secret life.

Share information about the widespread nature of abuse and how it is often kept a secret within close circles until it is often too late. Get students' feelings about abuse and whether they have experienced it or are aware of it or both. Ask students to give examples of both kinds of abuses and demonstrate examples through role playing.

Share information about a help hotline and shelters for victims and enforce that it is not enough. We need to enter the mind through education to stop the madness. This class is important. It represents an ongoing visual aid against domestic abuse.

Materials to be used for middle school

1. Teachers will use worksheets to aid in the understanding of physical and verbal abuse and allow a victim or one of the previously mentioned persons come in and give a lecture and leave time for questions and discussion.
2. Students will be asked to use the *library or Internet* throughout the grade period to stay abreast of evidence from victims, data gathered from different authors, and look for the root cause.
3. Serious discussions addressing how abuse can be eliminated and preparation for an escape.
4. Require students to keep a log to get in the habit of creating a paper trail (explain).

Assessment/Evaluation

1. Check logs.
2. Have students to visualize a long relationship with an abuser and plan an escape.
3. Written exam to make sure the students understand abusive behavior.

Materials that can be added for senior high school in addition to the middle school materials

1. Are there societies where abuse is more prevalent than other societies?
2. Are there societies where it is not prevalent at all?

3. Write a three-page typed paper using an outline to discuss abuse in different organized groups. Examples: Buddhism, Christianity, etc.

Some Data from the Internet on Abuse, from Personal Conversations, Research, and Experience

1. Abuse does not discriminate.[2]
2. Approximately 23 percent of the women in jail are victims who murdered the abuser.[3]
3. A woman is abused every fifteen seconds. [4]
4. The Christian woman is the least likely to get help (only 10 percent get help regardless of race).
5. Abuse is beginning with girls and boys as early as the sixth grade. (I know this from my research among schoolgirls in middle and high school.)
6. Abuse is a learned behavior. It is not innate.[5]
7. It is never the victim's fault, because someone else can do the same thing and the abuser does not react in the same fashion.[6]
8. Some women die thinking it was their fault to cause the abuse. (I know this from a conversation I had with a nurse who saw this happen when an elderly woman came to the hospital with broken ribs and pneumonia at seventy-six years old. She died thinking it was her fault. The patient kept saying, "I should not have made him mad. I am so sorry.")

National Teen Dating Abuse Helpline

Love Is Respect.org

When you start dating, don't ever think that the roughness exhibited is macho or cute. *As my dad would say, "Nip it in the bud."* Here are some signs to stop at inception! Don't make excuses for them, and please don't ignore them.

1. Does something about your partner not feel right?

---

2 Gelles, Richard J., edit. *Understanding Domestic Violence.* Rhode Island: University of Rhode Island Violence Research Program.

3 Ibid

4 Ibid

5 Matiagoss, Dr. Irene. "Sign of Verbal and Emotional Abuse." www.obgyn.net.

6 Ibid

2. Does your partner look at you or act in ways that scare you?
3. Does he or she act jealous or possessive?
4. Does he or she put you down or criticize you?
5. Does he or she try to control where you go, what you wear, or what you do?
6. Does he or she text you or IM you excessively?
7. Does he or she blame you for the hurtful things he or she says or does?
8. Does he or she threaten to kill or hurt you if you leave him or her?
9. Does he or she try to stop you from seeing or talking to friends and family?
10. Does he or she hit, slap, push, or kick you?

Fact Sheet on Battered Women in Prison

info@purpleberets.org

Women Compared to Men in Abusive Relationships

During my interaction with Women Of Excellence NWAS, Inc., I am being approached by more and more by men for us to do something for them also. I looked at some facts about men listed on a fact sheet on battered women in prison, and this is what I found.

1. As of now, it is estimated that 80 percent of women are abused, whereas 20 percent of men are abused. Any number is too many.
2. Currently there are two thousand battered women in America in prison for defending their lives against batterers, with the number being much smaller for men.
3. As many as 90 percent of those women in jail today for killing men had been battered by those men.
4. The average prison sentence of men who kill their women partners is two to six years. Women who kill their male partners are sentenced on the average to fifteen years, despite the fact that most women who kill do so in self-defense.

Two Other Good Sources for Information about Abuse

1. **Older Women in Prison—Hidden Victims of Domestic Violence**

www.allacademic.com/meta/p201201-indexhtml

2. **Understanding Domestic Violence Factoids**[7]

7 Gelles, Richard J. *Understanding Domestic Violence Factoids,* University of Rhode Island Violence Research Program. 1995.

Suggestions for a Short Presentation on Becoming a Woman of Excellence

WOMAN OF EXCELLENCE NOT WITHOUT A STRUGGLE

Woman—female gender[8]
Of—belonging to, aspiring to be, or belonging to something[9]
Excellence—distinction; degree of superiority[10]

Identified by:

a. actions
b. thoughts
c. appearance

Woe—heavy affliction; suffering[11]

To

Becoming a woman of excellence

You don't wake up one morning and say, "I am a woman of excellence." It is a process similar to a journey. The Bible states we are born in sin and shaped in iniquity (Psalm 51:5, KJV).

A. Be open-minded

1. Don't be afraid of change
2. Be a risk taker (self starter)
3. Set priorities
4. Set goals and follow through
5. Be a good listener
6. Be selective with the company you keep.

B. Develop a good prayer life

1. Know how to pray and get answers
2. Recognize the will of God in your answers

8 Landau, Sidney, edit, Webster's Dictionary. Chicago: J. G. Ferguson Publishing Company, 1978
9 Ibid
10 Ibid
11 Ibid

3. Trust God
4. Step out on faith

C. Never stop learning

1. Study to show yourself approved (2 Timothy 2:15 KJV).
2. "When there is better, good is not enough" (author unknown).

Please add your own dialogue. Add an introduction and conclusion to fit in with the occasion. The struggle is never over, but it gets better. Amen!

I certainly hope this information will be helpful.

Global Initiative

Eleven years ago when it came to me to write this book that started when I first left the abuser, my thoughts were to make this a national effort, but I know this needs to be a global initiative. When I see in the media where eight-year-old girls are being married off and not knowing it, that says to me that some females have no say as to what should happen to them. When judges uphold this behavior it grieves me deeply. When I see women all covered up peering through mesh I am grieved even more.

Something has to be done to stop the madness. This is abuse in the worst way. We must declare war on this behavior. It is not a concern for one group of women but for all women. *Abuse* does not discriminate. It has no boundaries when it comes to race, color, creed, or national origin. It transcends and cuts through all cultures, occupations, and income levels.

I have been trying to find a good spot to say this, and I think just before the epilogue is a good place. Aside from working hard to make a difference in the lives of women, I have one major desire for myself, and that is to conduct a large choir with at least one hundred voices. I have to contact someone to get training. I can hardly wait. Wish me well!

Epilogue

As this journey with me comes to an end, please don't feel sorry for me. Remember the many good years on the Travis place where a good foundation for family values were and other good things were laid. Growing up there was quite an experience. I wish the best for all the sharecroppers of the world and hope they will soon find freedom. This, too, is a form of abuse, which is a totally different story.

When you remember what I went through, in later years is what I thought was the right thing to do. Keeping abuse a secret and facing struggles without sharing them with anyone really take a toll on your body, personality, and relationships. I kept my secret struggles to myself for forty years and even forty days is much too long. My generation, among Christian women, was taught to stay with your husband because marriage vows are sacred. I talked to my mom without really telling her the whole story. When both my parents found out the entire story, neither would have encouraged me to stay in this horrible relationship. Mom and Dad loved each other. In our household, it was God first, spouses second, and children next. They didn't just say they loved each other, they showed it in so many ways. Mom was a beautiful, good, and wonderful wife, and his eight children were the best and the brightest. After we were grown and had left home, when we would return, friends and relatives were invited to come by to see us.

The drama was somewhat more intense than was spoken. Once there is family, it is never *I* again, it is always we. There is another person to be considered all the time if you are a good mother—a little life that needs Mom and Dad. If you have concluded that I was a nut by the time you came to this page in the book, you are wrong. I have excelled in so many things that my family, peers, and church family have raved about over the years. It was easy to get someone to work on my committees because they knew we would be successful. When I hear women say I can't see why a woman would put up with this, sadness like you wouldn't believe comes over me. To name a few reasons why I didn't leave earlier: embarrassment, concern about what someone would say, because of wedding vows being sacred, my thinking that the kids needed both parents and that Christian women don't leave their husbands readily, etc. I kept hoping that he would change or leave me since he would often accuse me of being such a bad person. I think love had something to do with the thoughts of leaving and the good times we had together (even though they were far fewer than the bad times). Some of my jobs paid much more than those of people with degrees, so I could have made it on my own. Finally, I didn't trust God enough to help me make it on my own or be whole by myself. I walked with Him daily and prayed daily but didn't trust Him enough to leave. I saw miracle after miracle and knew God was answering prayers but I allowed red flags and opportunities to evade me. Even though Oscar is dead, he is still missed at family functions. We still miss the barbecue. I still miss him although we had been apart for six years and six months before he died.

When I made up my mind to make the permanent exit, it was my first and foremost desire to save as many people as possible through the organization I started and an enhancement outline to introduce females as early as middle school. If used properly, without hesitation, it will prove vital to women and others in abusive relationships.

Our four children that I mentioned in my story, I don't know what I would have done without them. *Oscar III* married Charlotte Fleeton, is a talented musician who plays several instruments, and is a great graphic artist. He is the father of two super daughters, Docia Murphy Johnson and Tiffany, and grandfather of my first great-grandchild, Armani Kaniah Johnson. Docia is a senior in college, studying to be a research nurse, doing excellent, married and works at NASA as an internist. Docia married Immon Johnson (Bud), and he is stationed in Afghanistan. Tiffany is a senior in high school and doing very well and enjoys modeling and working for the summer. She is looking forward to attending college beginning in September 2010.

D'Vorolyn (Voe) married James Talley Jr., and he died at forty-two years old. She has worked for the Federal Bureau of Investigation for twenty-eight years. Together they had two sons, Jamerel (our miracle baby we call Jay), who was born three months and three weeks early, weighing only one pound and four ounces. Jay is twenty-two years old and is enjoying college, doing well, and working. Their second son is Javaughn and is a little genius and loves sports. He is all of our baby.

Sharolyn Murphy, Esq., a successful attorney who is a partner at Swartz Campbell Law Firm in Philadelphia, Pennsylvania, and is, according to her nieces and nephews, the best aunt in the world. I think every family should have a Sharolyn.

Wendolyn (Wendy) married Tim Cousin, and she works as an administrative assistant at Toras Chaim Orthodox School and loves it. Tim is a safety engineer and works as a supervisor at Jacob Industrial. They have two great children, a daughter, Karolyn, who is in college, doing outstanding, and working for the summer. Evan is in high school and is a good student. Evan says he is going to play pro football when he finishes college. We see the potential.

If you are getting ready for the pity party now, don't, put the tissues away. Today I wouldn't exchange the place where I am in life for anything. I retired June 1, 2003, and moved to my new home in Upper Marlboro, Maryland, to be near family, to a house that was built just for me. I have enjoyed giving it a special touch by decorating with ideas that I would love to have done in the house in Ohio. I am happy, and I am a lot like my dad and mom, and best of all, I am more like Christ and have grown closer to Him. I have joined Galilee Baptist Church in Suitland, Maryland and I am very happy there. Again, please don't feel sorry for me. I knew better. I stayed longer than I should have but didn't want to accept the fact that things would never change just because I am a Christian woman. I had seen a good marriage and had seen two people (Mom and Dad) who genuinely loved each other and walked together as one. I love my children, grandchildren, great-grandchild, sisters and brothers, and their families. I celebrate happiness *every day!* I thank God for the mom and dad God gave me. I thank Him for the children He gave me. If I had the opportunity to select my own children, I would pick the same four. I would definitely do some things differently, but I would select my same four. Dad died March 13, 2007, and there are a very few days when I am home that I don't call Mom. On Dad's death bed, one of his last request was and I quote, "Don't ever forget your mother, she has made a lot of sacrifices and has done a lot for all of us."

As I wrap things up, I am home visiting my mom. Thinking ahead, Mom will be ninety-three years old on August 2, 2010, and I will be seventy-three years old August 2, 2010. I was born on her twentieth birthday on a Monday. She is in fair health, and arthritis is decreasing her mobility slowly. We don't complain because we have so many things to be thankful for, so we celebrate life every single day. She goes through her favorite rituals—"Thank You, Lord, for waking me this morning. You didn't have to do it but You did. You woke me up with a reasonable portion of health and strength, clothed in my right mind, and I thank You for this day!" She has some other things that she says when some of her friends call. Father's Day will be coming soon and she has a list of things that she wants me to go to the cemetery and do for Dad's grave. As much as I hate to go there, I am going down to see what she wants done. Dad was a good man, an excellent father, an outstanding provider, and a pastor. Again, I know marriages can be healthy with love and respect for each other. People, *I saw one!* I admired it so much, I wanted one as close to their marriage as I could get.

Considering the awful household that my dad grew up in, and yet, he was such a very different person lets me know that these bad traits do not have to be passed down or mirrored. God and a willingness to love and treat people as you want to be treated makes all the difference in the world!

I hope you will use and refer back to the educational portion of the book. It contains factual information from an abuse survivor and from other reliable sources.

You will be hearing about me in the future more and more as I take on the task of globalizing the message about Women of Excellence NWAS, Inc., and what it stands for. The prevention of abuse in any form is more important than or as important as the cure. I want to get to the heart of women who are living with this monster and prevent others from wrestling with it now and in the future. I want to start early with the minds in middle school. You have a choice. Love yourself like you have never been loved before. Tell yourself that the abuser does not have a monopoly on happiness (or is it a love of control?). It belongs to everybody who chooses to grab it and say "It is mine to have, and I am not going to let you destroy it."

People tell me now that I was a very strong person to have endured such an intense relationship and endured such struggles ... I wonder.